No Substitute for Competence

ECPR Press

ECPR Press is an imprint of the European Consortium for Political Research. It publishes original research from leading political scientists and the best among early career researchers in the discipline. Its scope extends to all fields of political science, international relations, and political thought, without restriction in either approach or regional focus. It is also open to interdisciplinary work with a predominant political dimension.

ECPR Press Editors

Editors

Ian O'Flynn is Senior Lecturer in Political Theory at Newcastle University, UK.

Laura Sudulich is Reader in Public Policy at the University of Essex, UK. She is also affiliated to Cevipol (Centre d'Étude de la vie Politique) at the Université libre de Bruxelles, Belgium.

Associate Editors

Andrew Glencross is Senior Lecturer in the Department of Politics and International Relations at Aston University, UK.

Liam Weeks is Lecturer in the Department of Government and Politics, University College Cork, Ireland, and Honorary Senior Research Fellow, Department of Politics and International Relations, Macquarie University, Australia.

No Substitute for Competence

On the Origins and Consequences of Issue Ownership

Simon Lanz

Published by the European Consortium for Political Research, Harbour House, 6–8 Hythe Quay, Colchester, CO2 8JF, United Kingdom

British Library Cataloguing in Publication Data
A catalogue record for this book is available from the British Library

ISBN: HB 978-1-78552-344-1

Library of Congress Control Number: 2019952270

ISBN 978-1-78552-344-1 (cloth)
ISBN 978-1-5381-5688-9 (pbk)
ISBN 978-1-78552-345-8 (electronic)

ecpr.eu/shop

Contents

Acknowledgements

This project was made possible with the support of many people and institutions to whom I am indebted. First, I would like to thank my PhD supervisor Pascal Sciarini. He introduced me to the academic world and never got tired reading and commenting on the countless versions of the project. I also want to thank the other members of my great jury. Each meeting with Simon Hug led to several weeks of additional work. I still kept going back to ask for advice because his comments are always bulletproof. Nathalie Giger is an incredible mentor from both an academic and a personal perspective. She has provided invaluable support. Romain Lachat's research was another source of inspiration for my research. His inputs have been tough, but at the same time so relevant and rigorous that I have grown a lot as a researcher; thanks to them.

Thanks to the generous funding of the Swiss National Science Foundation (project no. P1GEP1 164874), I was able to spend a year as visiting scholar at the University of Mannheim hosted by Thomas Bräuninger. My stay at the University of Mannheim was without a doubt one of the greatest experiences of my professional life, thanks to the many encounters with brilliant researchers: Verena Fetscher, Christian Glässel, Belén González, Anna-Lena Hönig, Marcela Ibáñez, Ron David Lehrer, Moritz Marbach, Dominic Ponattu, Anne Schäfer, Adam Scharpf, Christian Schimpf, Michael Strebel, Tilko Swalve, and Jakob Willisch.

Upon return from Germany, I was hosted by the University of Bern, where I wrote large parts of the manuscript. I would like to express my gratitude to Markus Freitag for inviting me to work at the Institute of Political Science.

During the course of this project, I benefitted tremendously from the suggestions and inputs of many colleagues, among them Catherine de Vries,

Philipp Hunziker, Heike Klüver, Lucas Leemann, Alessandro Nai, Jonas Pontusson, Sergi Pardos-Prado, Anke Tresch, Fréderic Varone, and Markus Wagner.

I am further grateful to the colleagues and friends at the University of Geneva, with whom I shared the joys and frustrations of writing a PhD: Fabio Cappelletti, Fabian Cottier, Aurélien Evequoz, Julien Jaquet, Ivo Krizic, Nino Landerer, Davy-Kim Lascombes, Adrien Petitpas, Jan Rosset, Simone Wegmann, Lawrence Wiget, and Reto Wüest. In particular, I would like to mention my awesome (issue ownership) partner in crime, Alexandra Feddersen.

With Pirmin Bundi and Andreas Goldberg I have not only developed (and dismissed) countless ideas for new projects. We have also spent a lot of time playing and watching sports. Despite their poor taste in football teams, there was never a dull moment with the two of them. Speaking of sports, I would like to thank my friends Simon Bünzli and Benjamin Rupp for always making sure that I keep both feet on the ground by taking me out to climb high mountains.

In 2018, I have received a grant from the foundation 'Wissenschaftliche Politikstipendien', which made it possible for me to work at the Swiss Parliament. I am very grateful for this opportunity and for the support from my co-workers, especially Boris Burri, Christina Leutwyler, Rafael Schläpfer, Denise Campos, and Luciana Nanetti.

Finally, I would like to thank my wonderful family for their never-ending love and support. Mum, Dad, David, Mäthu, Ramona, Lars, Medina, Elias, Kasper, and Manuela: You are amazing! Above all, I would like to thank Deana, to whom I dedicate this book. Thank you for being in my life.z:

Abbreviations

GENERAL

BLM	Binary Logit Model
CHES	Chapel Hill Expert Survey
CI	Credibility interval
CLM	Conditional Logit Model
CMP	Comparative Manifestos Project
CPDS	Comparative Political Data Set
CSES	Comparative Study of Electoral Systems
EES	European Election Study
EU	European Union
FD	First difference
H	Hypothesis
HPD	Highest probability density region
IIA	Independence of irrelevant alternatives
It.	Iteration
MCMC	Markov chain Monte Carlo
MIP	Most important problem
MNAR	Missing not at random
MNLM	Multinomial Logit Model
N	Number of cases
NATO	The North Atlantic Treaty Organization
OECD	Organisation for Economic Co-operation and Development
OLS	Ordinary least squares
ÖVP	Austrian People's Party
ParlGov	Parliaments and governments database
Pr	Probability
PTV	Propensity to vote

Q   Question
SELECTS   Swiss Electoral Studies
SVP   Swiss People's Party
SPÖ   Social Democratic Party of Austria
TEV   True European Voter Project

COUNTRIES

AUS   Australia
AUT   Austria
CAN   Canada
CHE   Switzerland
CZE   Czech Republic
DEN   Denmark
EST   Estonia
FIN   Finland
FRA   France
GER   Germany
GRC   Greece
ICE   Iceland
ITA   Italia
NLD   Netherlands
NZL   New Zealand
NOR   Norway
POL   Poland
POR   Portugal
SVK   Slovakia
SVN   Slovenia
ESP   Spain
SWE   Sweden
UK   United Kingdom
USA   United States of America

Chapter 1

Introduction

"There is no substitute for competence." What is true in Ayn Rand's novel *The Fountainhead* (1943) must also apply to the realm of politics, one would think. If people want politicians getting things done, they surely elect the most competent[1] party for the job. And yet the argument that electoral decisions are linked to voters' assessments of party competence is fairly novel in the scholarly debate. This project contributes to the growing literature on "issue ownership voting" (Petrocik 1996: 833) or "competence-based voting" (Green 2007: 646). It argues that in politics too, nothing substitutes competence.

Issue ownership is a tale of two actors. On the one hand, it theorizes how *parties* compete with each other in their struggle for votes. It claims that each party has a reputation for competence on a specific political topic (Budge and Farlie 1983). They can win elections by getting their issue at the top of the public agenda (Petrocik 1996). In the process, parties reframe issues into goals shared by the whole society. They hide policy trade-offs and avoid confrontation with rival parties on the same issue (De Sio and Weber 2014).

On the other hand, issue ownership is about the *citizen*. Over the past forty-five years, scholars have repeatedly found that voters are more likely to support a party if they think it is competent to handle issues they care about (Bellucci 2006; Kuechler 1991; Nadeau et al. 2001; RePass 1971).

However, the mechanism behind issue ownership voting is still undertheorized. In an attempt to clarify the links between competence and the vote, I will claim that issue ownership voting consists of three assumptions: first, voters are primarily interested in having issues handled by a competent party. Unlike in other issue voting models, this implies that voters are reluctant (or unable) to deal with the specificities of the exact solution to a political problem. Though positional considerations feed into evaluations of party

1

competence, other factors are important, too. Hence the second assumption, following which issue-handling competence is a subjective preference with various sources. Third, competence is more decisive in the decision-making process if the voter cares deeply about the issue. These three assumptions yield the following formula of issue ownership voting: *voters support the most competent party on the most important issue.*

Although research on issue ownership voting is evolving quickly, many questions remain unanswered. First, the origins of party competence ratings are understudied. In this respect, issue ownership differs from other theories of electoral behaviour, where the key explanatory variables have come under scrutiny. Most contributions simply repeat John R. Petrocik's famous statement that ownership is produced by a party's "history of attention" on an issue (1996: 826). Those who delve deeper into the subject have found individual-level issue ownership to be a multifaceted concept (e.g. Therriault 2015). Some argue that parties can manipulate ownership through either issue attention (Meguid 2005) or good performance while in government (Petrocik 1996). Others argue that ownership is mostly a product of partisanship and voter-party distance (Walgrave et al. 2016). Thus far, no study has investigated these four sources simultaneously in multiple countries.[2]

This relates to a second shortcoming of the literature. Research on competence-based voting is to an astonishing degree non-comparative. Following Lefevere et al., "the contemporary literature on issue ownership is overwhelmingly national" (2017: 3). In fact, it is not only national, it centres around a handful of Western European countries (mostly Belgium, Denmark, the Netherlands, Switzerland, and the UK). Notable exceptions are Kuechler (1991) and Pardos-Prado (2012), both of whom studied the competence-based voting in the context of the European Parliament elections. This narrow focus is problematic since it remains unclear if issue ownership voting is a universal driver of the vote choice or if it applies only to an exclusive group of countries.

The third gap concerns the near absence of contextual variables in issue ownership research. According to Curtice, "We cannot expect to understand elections and electoral behaviour simply by looking at them through the prism of the voter" (2002: 165). But this is exactly what current research on competence-based voting is doing. Clearly this is a consequence of the aforementioned focus on single-country analyses. Nevertheless, besides the cross-national studies by Kuechler (1991) and Pardos-Prado (2012), two further contributions exploit either the contextual variation within a country (Lachat 2011) or across time (Green and Hobolt 2008). These authors have come to conflicting conclusions with regard to the moderating effect of party system fragmentation and polarization. The role of other contextual factors has not been analysed thus far. I propose to link research on clarity of responsibility (Powell and Whitten 1993) with the issue ownership voting.

A final weakness regards methodological strategies used in the field. Until a decade ago, and in exceptional cases to this day, it was common to investigate issue ownership voting with aggregate-level data. The best-known example for this is Petrocik (1996), whose finding that US presidential candidates perform better when their issues dominate the public agenda is based on aggregated vote shares from nine elections. Furthermore, it is surprisingly rare to find studies on the impact of competence evaluations on the vote choice in national legislative elections (but see Bellucci 2006; Green and Hobolt 2008). Some (e.g. Lachat 2014; Pardos-Prado 2012; van der Brug 2004) approximate the voters' so-called propensity to vote (PTV), which indicates how probable a citizen is to ever vote for a party (van der Eijk et al. 2006). While this variable has been quite frequently employed in electoral research, the models used to predict PTVs have been criticized recently (e.g. Giger and Hug 2018). Whatever position one takes on this matter, these scores are, per definition, not the same thing as the actual vote choice. Other studies estimate issue ownership voting by running hierarchical logistic regressions on a stacked dataset where each observation represents a voter/party combination (e.g. Walgrave, Lefevere, and Tresch 2012). This likely produces flawed results since the observations are not independent from each other.

The aim of this project is to remedy these shortcomings. It centres around the following research questions:

Q1:   *To what extent do partisanship, voter-party distance, party performance, and party issue attention determine individual competence ratings?*

Q2:   *To what extent do voters base their decisions on evaluations of party issue competence?*

Q3:   *To what extent do polarization, fragmentation, and clarity of responsibly explain variation in issue ownership voting?*

By tackling these questions, this book seeks to advance the scholarly debate and to further our understanding of the voting process. The study will first confirm that party issue competence has multiple sources. Partisanship and voter-party distance emerge as the most influential drivers of such evaluations. In some countries, parties can shape their reputation by spending more attention on an issue than their rivals. Furthermore, except for a few democracies, assessments of competence are linked to government performance. This indicates that parties can, to some extent, influence their ownership in the short run and use it as a tool to gain votes. Second, the study sheds light on the decision-making process in national legislative elections. Issue ownership voting is present in the entire sample of democracies. More importantly, the theory adds to existing models of the vote choice, most notably partisanship voting, proximity voting, and performance voting. The role of competence is more pronounced for nonpartisans and voters who are not positionally close to the party. Third, this study theorizes and analyses how the political context moderates issue ownership voting. It will underscore that competence-based voting is a universal phenomenon. However, it appears to be most prevalent in highly fragmented systems. From a party perspective, this means that being regarded as capable of handling an important issue is always a desirable goal, no matter which election the party competes in.

The project makes contributions beyond these findings. It develops a theoretical and an empirical framework to measure the origins and conse-quences of party competence. Using individual-level data from the Compara-tive Study of Electoral Systems (CSES), it predicts party choice with fully specified hybrid regression models. These models bypass stacking the data or using the 'propensity-to-vote' as outcome by simultaneously estimating effects of voter-specific and party-specific indicators on the vote choice. The sample consists of twenty-four advanced democracies. In most of these countries, competence-based voting has never been tested in the context of a national legislative election.

In a general sense, this study is about the functioning of political systems. It deals with a central element of modern democratic societies. Against the backdrop of increasing partisan dealignment and voter volatility, Russell Dalton has proclaimed the age of cognitive mobilization in which citizens rely less on partisan cues and instead act as "independent issue voters" (1984: 282). In this view, issue voting is the prerogative of the well informed. In competence-based voting, this is not necessarily the case. Issue ownership voters do not have to compare party positions on a large number of issues (Lachat 2011: 647). At low cognitive costs, the theory advances a type of voting where "politics is about policy" (Alvarez and Nagler 1998: 56). This is important because, following Ole Borre, "the idea of issue voting is that of society taking control of its own destiny" (2001: 9). This project shows that voters are not indifferent towards political issues. They want to see competent people handling the problems they care about. Evaluations of party compe-tence affect the vote choice beyond partisanship, proximity, and performance voting. As I will demonstrate in the following pages, the claim that nothing substitutes competence is more than fiction.

This study is divided into seven parts. Chapter 2 reviews the literature on the role of issue perceptions in electoral behaviour. It introduces the three classical models of voting and situates issue ownership within the rational choice framework. It further presents the main contributions in the field of party-level and voter-level issue ownership and summarizes some of the more recent developments. Chapter 3 presents my theoretical assumptions and hypotheses. It first identifies four sources of individual party competence evaluations. It then turns to the mechanism of issue ownership voting and introduces two individual-level moderators. In a final step, it discusses how competence-based voting is expected to vary across different party systems and government compositions. Chapter 4 describes the case selection, the data, and the statistical framework. It, moreover, describes in detail how each concept is measured.

The first empirical chapter investigates the sources of party competence ratings (chapter 5). It sheds light on how such evaluations are driven by partisanship, voter-party distance, party performance, and issue attention. Chapter 6 analyses issue ownership voting in twenty-four democracies and explores if it is moderated by partisanship and voter-party distance. Chapter 7 addresses the interplay between the political context and the competence-based voting. It tests conflicting hypotheses on the role of party system polarization and fragmentation and provides a very first analysis of issue ownership voting across different levels of clarity of responsibility.

Chapter 8 gives a final summary of the results and discusses their implications for party competition and the scholarly debate on electoral behaviour. It further states the limitations of the study and points out avenues for future research.

Chapter 2

Perspectives on Issue Voting and Issue Ownership Voting

Because this election is not about ideology. It's about competence. It's not about overthrowing governments in Central America; it's about creating jobs in middle America. That's what this election is all about.
Michael S. Dukakis, Democratic National Convention in Atlanta, 21 July 1988

The aim of this chapter is to give an overview of the relevant literature and to prepare the stage for the theoretical framework. It is structured as follows: I first discuss how the classic schools of electoral research theorize the origins of issue opinions and their role in the decision-making process. In the Columbia and the Michigan studies, issue preferences take a back seat. They are overshadowed by either group membership or party identification (section 2.1). Rational choice theory, on the other hand, highlights the importance of issues in elections and serves as the theoretical basis of most issue voting approaches (section 2.2). In section 2.3, I turn to issue ownership research and introduce the cornerstone studies by Budge and Farlie (1983) and Petrocik (1996). This literature is primarily concerned with party behaviour and has been coined the "aggregate-level issue ownership theory" (Bélanger and Meguid 2008: 477).[1] The voter-level component is introduced in section 2.4.

This research centres on Bellucci's claim that citizens support parties, which they rate competent to deal with a political issue (2006). Over the past decade, the issue ownership model has become more elaborated. Section 2.5 discusses refinements of the ownership concept (associative versus competence ownership and the dynamics of issue ownership), as well as important moderators of issue ownership voting (issue salience and the political context). In section 2.6, I point out open questions and give an outlook over the next steps.

2.1 THE COLUMBIA MODEL AND THE MICHIGAN MODEL

In the beginning of the 1940s, Paul Lazarsfeld, Bernard Berelson, and Hazel Gaudet collaborated on a project which is perceived to be the foundation of modern electoral research (Bartels 2010). The backbone of the so-called Columbia study is a series of surveys conducted entirely in one municipality in the United States (Erie County, Ohio). Lazarsfeld, Berelson, and Gaudet published their findings in *The People's Choice: How the Voter Makes Up His Mind in a Presidential Campaign* (1944). Ten years later, the same research group conducted a second study resulting in *Voting: A Study of Opinion Formation in a Presidential Campaign* (Berelson, Lazarsfeld, and McPhee 1954). Both contributions constitute the core of what is commonly referred to as the *micro sociological approach*. At the outset, the researchers wanted to examine changing party preferences, which they expected to be volatile and affected by the media. However, their results showed that the vote choice is stable over time and determined by group membership. Citizens with a high socioeconomic status were more prone to support the Republicans than the Democrats. While Protestants usually voted Republican, Catholics tended to vote Democratic (Lazarsfeld, Berelson and Gaudet 1944: chapter 2). The translation of social structures into party preferences is almost deterministic and leaves little room for issue-based voting. In contrast to the other classical theories of voting behaviour, issue evaluations are linked with group membership and characterized by stability.

In a development of the theory, the *macrosociological approach*, Lipset and Rokkan (1967) claimed that party systems mirror countries' cleavage structures. Following Bartolini and Mair, social cleavages contain an empirical, a normative, and an organizational element (1990: 199). The empirical element describes a societal division. The groups, moreover, hold common values (normative element) which are articulated on the organizational level (organizational element). This means that issue preferences are not determined by the citizens' position in the social structure. Quite the opposite, they play a crucial role in the emergence and continuance of cleavages. Note that the theory uses the term 'values'. While values are conceptually different from issues, they are empirically related (for a similar argument, see Giger 2011).[2]

The second classical theory of political behaviour is the *sociopsychological model* (also Michigan study or Ann Arbor approach). According to Bartels (2010: 242), the principal output of this theory, *The American Voter* (Campbell et al. 1960), turned out to be nothing less than "the most important landmark in the whole canon of electoral research". *The American Voter* conceptualizes the vote as the product of a chain of events, which can be pictured as a "funnel of causality" (Campbell et al. 1960: 24). Long-term elements such as the cleavage structure are located at the mouth of the funnel. Short-term elements like attitudes towards candidates or issue preferences are at the stem of the funnel. In this view, party identification has a pivotal intermediary position: "Few factors are of greater importance for our national elections than the lasting attachment of tens of millions of Americans to one of the parties" (Campbell et al. 1960: 121). Party identification is defined as a psychological affinity to a political party in the individual's environment. It is acquired in the pre-adult years through the process of political socialization (see also Hyman 1959). In this phase, the social milieu, mostly the family, passes its political beliefs to the next generation. While partisan loyalties are characterized by stability, they occasionally can change over time (see also Converse 1969; Jennings 2007; Jennings and Niemi 1981; Miller and Shanks 1996).

To a limited extent, the theory acknowledges the existence of issue voting. Issue preferences are highly volatile attitudes towards ongoing political problems like education spending, external relations, the influence of big business in politics, or the firing of suspected communists (Campbell et al. 1960: 101). Such preferences mostly come into play when researchers have to explain the dynamic part of an election (i.e. when party identification fails to predict the vote choice). "It is *not* true that attitudes toward the several elements of politics are only reflections of party loyalty or group membership. . . . To suppose that they are is to understate the importance of changes in the properties of what the individual sees in his environment. . . . The truth of this statement is easily seen if we observe that attitudes toward the objects of politics, varying through time, can explain short-term fluctuations in partisan division of the vote, whereas party loyalties and social characteristics, which are relatively inert through time, account but poorly for these shifts" (Campbell et al. 1960: 65). Generally, issue voting takes place if three conditions are met: first, the voter has to be familiar with the issue. Second, issues should produce feelings that are held with a certain level of intensity. Third, voters have to be capable of identifying a party that presents the best solutions to the problem.

2.2 THE RATIONAL CHOICE MODEL OF VOTING

The third classical theory of electoral behaviour was popularized by Anthony Downs in *An Economic Theory of Democracy* (1957). The *rational choice theory of voting* draws an analogy between democracies and economic markets. Every day, citizens receive goods from the government. They drink purified water, walk on maintained streets, swim in public pools, and send their kids to schools. Following Downs, government action benefits can be reduced to a common denominator called 'utility'. Since voters are rational actors,[3] they cast the ballot for the party they believe will provide them the highest utility. This means that electorate does not care about policies "*per se*" (Downs 1957: 42, emphasis in original) but about how policies affect their utility income. Building on studies by statistician Hotelling (1929) and psychologist Coombs (1950), Downs develops the *proximity model of voting*, which is based on three assumptions: first, each citizen is represented by a point in a political space so that the point reflects the policies providing him or her with the highest utility. Second, party positions can be summarized in the same space. Third, voters select the party closest to their own position. Over the past years, many have provided empirical support for the proximity model (e.g. Alvarez 1997; Baker, Dalton, and Hildebrandt 1981; Enelow and Hinich 1984; Irwin and van Holsteyn 1989; Lacy and Paolino 1998; Page and Jones 1979; Rose and McAllister 1986). Alvarez and Nagler even go so far as to call it the "dominant paradigm in the voting literature, . . . supplanting the funnel of causality which had a brief reign beginning around 1960" (1998: 55).

Rabinowitz and Macdonald (1989: 93) propose an alternative spatial approach – the *directional model of issue voting*. This model is guided by two ideas (see also Macdonald, Listhaug, and Rabinowitz 1991; Macdonald, Rabinowitz, and Listhaug 1997; Maddens 1996): First, voters favour parties on the same side of the neutral point over all parties on the other side of the neutral point. Second, when deciding among different parties on their side of the neutral point, voters like extreme positions more than moderate positions. Finding the superior spatial model of vote choice has been one of the most inspiring puzzles in the voting literature (Macdonald, Rabinowitz, and Listhaug 1998; Westholm 1997). The majority of studies find strong evidence for the proximity model but little for the directional model. For instance, Tomz and Van Houweling (2008) claim that proximity voting is four times as common as directional voting. Claassen (2009) posits that the decision-making strategy is conditional on the policy area. While abortion-based evaluations are primarily directional, opinions about military spending stimulate proximity voting. Despite this evidence, declaring a winner has proven to be an impossible task. As Lewis and King (1999) demonstrate, too much depends on untestable assumptions both camps make when defending their case.

The counterpart of spatial models is the *valence model of voting*, developed by Donald Stokes (1963; 1985; 1992). He observed that the top issues in most elections are characterized by agreement. This is at odds with spatial models, where voters (and parties) take different stands on an issue. Stokes proposes to distinguish two types of issues: *position issues* are problems on which parties disagree over the goal. As for these issues, parties can be differentiated on ideology, which is required for spatial models to work. On *valence issues*, parties share the same goal but disagree over the way to achieve it.[4] In this case, proximity or directional voting is no longer possible: "The machinery of the spatial model will not work if the voters are simply reacting to the association of the parties with some goal or state or symbol that is positively or negatively valued" (Stokes 1963: 373).[5] This is important for political parties as well as for the voters. Instead of changing their policy position, parties emphasize their competence in achieving a shared goal (De Sio and Weber 2014: 871). In the voting process, valence evaluations such as issue performance or issue-handling competence take over the role of positional proximity (Clarke et al. 2004). However, the view that competence evaluations are only important in the context of valence issues has been challenged. According to van der Brug (2017: 533), "The largest threat to the reputation occurs when incumbent parties mess up on an issue about which opposition parties have proposed alternative lines of government action."

Nevertheless, several issue ownership studies have picked up the distinction between valence and position issues. van der Brug excludes position issues *ex-ante* (2004). Green and Hobolt (2008) find that party competence ratings matter more in elections that are primarily fought over valence issues. That is, if position issues are at the top of the public agenda, proximity emerges as the most influential driver of party choice. Bélanger and Meguid (2008) use competence evaluations on valence issues (increasing the number of jobs and fighting crime) and position issues (cutting taxes and preserving social programs) to approximate the voting decision. They argue that valence issues should not yield direct effects on the vote choice. "If an individual does not share a party's issue stance, then it is irrelevant that she finds that particular party to be the owner of the policy position" (Bélanger and Meguid 2008: 483). In other words, party competence ratings should only affect party support when the positions of the voter and the party are close. However, while this reasoning is in line with the Stokesian framework, their empirical results hardly justify a clear separation of valence and position issues.

The spatial models and the valence model are in many ways irreconcilable. Nevertheless, they share a common view of the voting citizen in that they posit that policy is the motor of politics. That is, issue preferences and party preferences are strongly linked. This sets this line of research apart from the Columbia model or the Michigan model, where decisions are driven by long-term determinants such as group-belonging or partisanship. Over the past decades, issue voting research has experienced an important upswing. This is arguably the scholarly reaction to the growing electoral volatility in Western democracies (e.g. Crewe and Denver 1985; Dalton, Flanagan, and Beck 1984; Franklin 1985). In a seminal study, Russell Dalton argued that this voter volatility is the product of a "cognitive mobilization" (1984: 264). Due to higher levels of education, a growing share of the electorate no longer depends on party cues. Instead, these "apartisans have the potential to act as . . . independent issue voters" (Dalton 1984: 282). Besides the spatial model and the valence model, issue ownership is a third theory linking issues with the vote choice.

2.3 PARTY-LEVEL ISSUE OWNERSHIP

Budge and Farlie's *Explaining and Predicting Elections: Issue Effects and Party Strategies in Twenty-Three Democracies* (1983) is the first comprehensive study on the mechanisms of issue ownership on the party level.[6] The underlying assumption of the theory is that some parties benefit more from a public debate on a given topic than others do. If party *a*'s issue is hardly present in the news and party *b*'s issue is highly debated, party *b* will most likely win the election. To take advantage of this mechanism, parties do not compete on all political issues. They focus on problems that are beneficial to them and hurtful to their adversaries. Let us assume that party *a* is best known for expanding welfare services. In this case, *a* will try to advance this issue because it can be sure that a better and more comprehensive welfare service will be appreciated by most voters. On the flip side, policies expanding welfare services are costly and result in unpopular tax increases. Including both issues in the campaign means talking about a policy that benefits a better part of the electorate (welfare issues) and a policy that hurts a majority of the voters (tax increases). Party *a*, thus, evokes positive and negative feelings among the electorate. This can be avoided by sticking solely to the issue where *a* has the reputation of benefitting a large share of the voters. Linking issues can reveal weak spots and should be avoided at all costs. The strategy of *talking past each other* is a fundamental difference to the valence model (Stokes 1963), where parties compete with each other to gain an image of competence on an issue.

An important element of the theory is the distinction of issues with and without "fixed effects" (Budge and Farlie 1983: 48). Most issues have fixed effects, meaning that they are beneficial to one specific party. However, the effects of 'government record' and 'foreign relations' are situation-specific, which means that no party can truly own these issues. The question if an issue has a fixed effect is important for the duration of ownership. Issues with a fixed direction are owned in the long run. Ownership over issues without fixed direction, on the other hand, is short term and depends on a party's current performance and its incumbency status. In terms of citations, Budge and Farlie's study is only surpassed by John Petrocik's *Issue Ownership in Presidential Elections, with a 1980 Case Study* (1996). A key innovation of this analysis is the conceptualization of issue ownership. Following Budge and Farlie, issue ownership is linked to benefits voters can expect when a party is able to pursue its policies. In this sense, issue ownership is an expression of the voters' self-interest. In Petrocik's view, issue ownership indicates that a party is regarded more competent to handle an issue than its opponents: "Handling is the ability to resolve a problem of concern to voters. It is a reputation for policy and program interests, produced by a history of attention, initiative, and innovation toward these problems, which prompts voters to believe that one of the parties (and its candidates) is more sincere and committed to doing something about them" (1996: 862). This implies that issue ownership is a long-term achievement, unlikely to change between two elections.[7]

Similar to Budge and Farlie, Petrocik shows that ownership can be volatile. Issues where this is the case are labelled 'performance issues', because ownership comes from the *record of the incumbent* party. Challengers can lease short-term ownership if they blame the government for handling a performance issue poorly. Petrocik's list of performance issue includes "the economy, the conduct of foreign relations, and the functioning of the government" (1996: 827, emphasis in original). However, the definition of the concept remains ambiguous and sometimes at odds with empirical findings (see section 3.1.2).

But what precisely is the role of issue ownership in party competition? Since issue ownership is primarily a long-term achievement, election campaigns are not oriented towards gaining new ownership. Rather, they are "marketing efforts" (Petrocik 1996: 828), where parties aim to put an owned issue in the centre of the attention. The author tests this by analysing *The New York Times* articles published during the month prior to nine American presidential elections. The result shows that in their speeches, candidates concentrate on issues owned by their respective party. With some variation of strength, this effect is observed in all elections and for both parties.

In conclusion, the differences between Petrocik and the study by Budge and Farlie are fairly small. Parties own political issues in the long run. The dynamic element of the theories is issue importance and not issue ownership (except in the case of performance issues or issues without fixed effects). If a party succeeds in increasing the importance of an issue, voters will turn to this party on the election day. Most subsequent studies have investigated the party-level component of the theory (e.g. Benoit and Hansen 2004; Green-Pedersen 2007; Hayes 2005; Klingemann, Hofferbert, and Budge 1994; Meguid 2005; Petrocik, Benoit, and Hansen 2003; Sellers 1998; Simon 2002). A principal question this research has focused on is to what degree parties confront each other on the same issues (Budge, Robertson and Hearl 1987; Damore 2004; Robertson 1976; Sides 2006). Whether a successful campaign strategy includes talking about issues owned by a competing party remains unclear. While Norpoth and Buchanan (1992) or Holian (2004) doubt that the so-called issue trespassing pays off electorally, Hayes (2005) underscores potential benefits.

2.4 CLASSIC STUDIES OF VOTER-LEVEL ISSUE OWNERSHIP

In a 1971 article, David RePass challenged the paradigm that issues play a negligible role in the decision-making process. He argued that closed-ended questions, where participants are confronted with a predefined list of issues, are the central problem of previous research attempts. In order to ascertain how issues affect decisions, scholars should measure how important these issues are to the voter. The way to achieve this is with open-ended questions enquiring about the most pressing problem. According to RePass, the superiority of this question is evidenced by the pronounced temporal change in issue-related attitudes. To him, open-ended issue questions overcome the problem of simply copying long-term party identification. He further observed remarkable differences between the perceived competence of parties to handle certain issues. The Democratic Party is preferred to deal with Medicare, social security, and aid for the poor. The Republicans are competent on foreign aid and fiscal policy. The analysis, moreover, shows that partisans not always consider their party as the most competent to handle the most important problem (MIP). In many cases, the perceived issue-handling competence prevails over long-term party attachment: "The remarkable thing that emerges from this analysis is that *salient issues had almost as much weight as party identification in predicting voting choice*" (RePass 1971: 400, emphasis in the original).

Kuechler (1991) was the second forerunner of issue ownership voting research. Comparing different European countries, he distinguishes voters with homogeneous and heterogeneous competence evaluations. Respondents were asked to evaluate issue-handling competence on the three most pressing political problems. Citizens who named the same party competent on all issues are classified as having *homogeneous competence opinions* and those who named at least two different parties as having *heterogeneous competence opinions*. To assess the impact of competence evaluation on the vote, Kuechler measured if the most competent party matches the elected party (i.e. matching vote choice). He shows that homogeneous opinions seldom come with nonmatching vote intentions. Voters with heterogeneous perceptions tended to vote for the most competent party to solve the top issue. The author concludes, "For the most part then, party competence evaluations are in line with voting intentions. Still, the segment of non-matching voters is large enough to warrant further analysis" (Kuechler 1991: 97).

The author then turns to the sociodemographic characteristics of issue ownership voters. Nonmatching voters are hypothesized to display high interest in politics as they decide more carefully and weigh different pieces of information before deciding. The results show that citizens with close party ties more often display a match between competence evaluation and the vote than citizens without party identification. However, this effect varies in strength and direction between the countries in the analysis. Nonmatching voters are most frequent among those who feel very close to a party. This leaves the author puzzled. Further, no pattern seems to emerge for the hypotheses on political interest, political information, education, and ideology.

Petrocik (1996) gives further insights into how issue ownership affects individual decision-making. Based on a newspaper content analysis, he measures the dominance of Democratic-owned issues in nine presidential elections and plots it against the success of Democratic candidates. The results show a strong relationship between the two variables and thus support the claim that voters support the candidate who owns the top issue. This indicates how the median voter must be characterized: while he or she is inclined to view elections as an opportunity to resolve problems, he or she is reluctant to deal with the specifics of a solution and to impose ideological consistency on issues: "The key fact for this voter is not what policies candidates promise to pursue, but what problems . . . will be resolved" (Petrocik 1996: 830).

Nadeau et al. (2001) analyse the effect of issue ownership in Canadian national elections. Compared to previous contributions, the authors propose a different definition of issue ownership. They use the term "images of parties" (2001: 1), which refers to the recognized capacity to handle competently certain issues and problems. At the same time, issue ownership is referred to as a "party's reputation" (2001: 1), which contains two dimensions. First, a certain number of adversaries have to recognize another party's competence in a policy field. This dimension is measured by looking at how much the perceived handling competence of an issue exceeds the vote shares of a party. The advantage of this method should be that the share of issue ownership that is the mere product of partisanship is filtered out. If competence is solely dependent on party identification, the difference between vote share and issue ownership should be zero. Second, the reputation of a party depends on its performance when in power. Different than in Petrocik (1996), performance ownership is long term. For example, the economic policies of the Hoover administration gave the Republicans the long-lasting reputation of being the "party of hard times" (Nadeau et al. 2001: 2). The pathbreaking idea of the contribution is to include individual perceptions of competence in a model of vote choice. The analysis demonstrates that party competence ratings play an important role in the decision-making beyond partisanship. Voters supported parties they considered apt to handle certain issues.[8]

Van der Brug (2004) is more critical towards individual-level effects of issue ownership voting. His research is explicitly motivated by the decreasing explanatory power of sociological models (see Dalton 1996; Franklin 1992) and the subsequent rise of literature on short-term explanatory variables (Alvarez 1997; Alvarez and Nagler 1995: 9; Rose and McAllister 1986). Van der Brug criticizes this literature for focusing only position issues. In light of this, he develops a new model where he examines the impact of valence issues on the vote.[9] The model includes information on the citizens' and the parties' issue priorities and estimates issue ownership voting similar to a standard proximity model. A first test confirms that voters are more likely to support a party if their issue priorities are in line. However, overlapping priorities explain only a fraction of the party preferences.[10] While convergent issue priorities statistically increase the voting utility, the effect appears to be substantially weak. Overall, the findings are disappointing: "issue priorities have little power to explain *individual* party preferences" (van der Brug 2004: 221, emphasis in the original). A likely explanation for this upshot is the way the author operationalizes issue ownership. The variable is similar to recent measures of *associative issue ownership*, which refers to the association of a party with a specific political problem (see section 2.5). Most studies on associative ownership show that this type of issue ownership does not have a direct effect on the vote choice (Lachat 2014; Walgrave, Lefevere, and Tresch 2014). Due to this "unusual operationalization", Bélanger and Meguid question the reliability and the generalizability of the results (2008: 479).

A further cornerstone study on issue ownership voting is Bellucci's contribution 'Tracing the Cognitive and Affective Roots of Party Competence' (2006). He investigates the cases of Italy and Great Britain and builds on previous findings showing that competence in economic issues is a key variable in explaining a party's electoral success (Bellucci and Bull 2002; Evans 1999; Sanders et al. 2001). According to Bellucci, issue ownership can be (but does not have to be) short term and describes a party's capacity to deliver policies. The empirical test regresses answers on the MIP and the party most competent to solve the problem against the vote choice. The findings show that issue salience and competence evaluations have a direct effect on the vote choice. However, among the two variables, competence is more crucial and dampens the effects of salience: "The introduction of party competence in the model has a clear depressing impact on issues, and in both countries fewer issues retain an independent direct effect on voting, while party competence shows strong effects" (Bellucci 2006: 552).

Bellucci's proposition is the quintessential issue ownership voting model according to which voters base their decision on perceptions of a party's competence to handle an issue.

2.5 RECENT REFINEMENT OF THE ISSUE OWNERSHIP VOTING MODEL

The ever-growing interest in the micro-foundations of issue ownership has led to a *fine-grained conceptualization of ownership*. While there is reluctance to settle on a common definition, most scholars agree that ownership is the "link between specific parties and issues in the minds of voters" (Walgrave, Tresch, and Lefevere 2015: 778). In most studies, including the present one, this link is about competence. Simply put, *competence ownership* is a voter's perception regarding a party's competence to solve a specific political problem. Recently, several scholars have introduced a second type of issue ownership (Kleinnijenhuis and Walter 2014; Lachat 2014; Lutz and Sciarini 2016; Tresch, Lefevere, and Walgrave 2015; Walgrave, Lefevere, and Tresch 2012; Walgrave et al. 2016). *Associative ownership* describes the "spontaneous association between an issue and a party . . ., regardless of whether voters consider the party to be the most competent to deal with this issue" (Walgrave, Lefevere, and Tresch 2014: 1). As becomes clear from this definition, associative and competence ownerships do not necessarily coincide. For instance, a voter might associate the immigration issue with a right-wing party without thinking that the party is best in handling the issue.[11] In the first systematic study on associative issue ownership, Walgrave, Lefevere, and Tresch (2012) confirm that voters often spontaneously associate issues with a party and that these associations are often different from their competence assessment. Moreover, associative ownership does not influence the vote choice directly, unless it regards a highly important issue. Similarly, in Switzerland, Lachat (2014) does not find that associative issue ownership increases the expected utility for a party. However, associative ownership moderates the proximity model of voting by highlighting the effects of spatial distance on party preference: "The expected effects of associative ownership are linked with the higher accessibility of the corresponding issue considerations in voters' minds" (2014: 739). An analysis of the Swiss elections confirms that competence ownership has a direct effect on decision-making; associative ownership, however, does not impact the vote choice (Lutz and Sciarini 2016).

One of the most important innovations was *adding issue salience* to the issue ownership voting model. This element is already present in early studies of competence-based voting (Bellucci 2006; RePass 1971). However, Bélanger and Meguid (2008) are the first to provide a detailed analysis of the role issue salience plays in issue ownership voting. They argue that ownership should only affect the vote choice of those who think that the issue is important: "Indeed, why should knowing that the Democrats . . . are the owner of the health care issue matter for an individual's vote if she thinks that health care is an irrelevant issue." Bélanger and Meguid estimate how party competence on four issues affects the probability to support the five Canadian parties. They show that the effect of competence evaluation on a given issue is significant in five out of twenty cases when the issue is unimportant.[12] If the issue is moderately important, the number of significant positive effects increases to fourteen. Finally, party competence ratings have a significant effect in sixteen out of twenty cases if the issue is perceived as highly salient. These findings underscore the pivotal role of salience in issue ownership voting.

Over the past years, various studies have *analysed the dynamic nature of issue ownership*. In classic contributions, ownership is conceptualized as fairly stable over time. According to Petrocik (1996: 826), "Perceptions of a party's issue competence probably change very slowly, when they change at all." This is in line with Seeberg (2016), who finds that "issue ownership appears quite stable across time and quite similar across countries" (2016: 14). In the case of the United States, Egan (2013) comes to a similar conclusion. However, other authors have pointed out that aggregate issue ownership might be more volatile than presumed (Bélanger 2003; Brasher 2009; Green and Jennings 2012a; Nadeau et al. 2001; Petitpas and Sciarini 2018; Tresch and Feddersen 2019). This view gains support from several voter-level analyses. In a survey experiment, Walgrave, Lefevere, and Nuytemans (2009) show that exposure to news reports can prompt people to shift their perception of a party's issue-handling competence. Similarly, Aalberg and Jenssen's quasi-experiment demonstrates that television debates exert a short-term effect on party issue competence evaluations of Norwegian first-time voters (2007). Kleinnijenhuis and Walter (2014) confirm the impact of election news on associative issue ownership. The authors find that instability in voters' spontaneous associations between issues and parties on the individual level goes hand in hand with stability in associative issue ownership on the aggregate level. In a further study, Walgrave and Lefevere (2017) look at the drivers of changing issue ownership perceptions in Belgium. They find that party characteristics as well as individual factors are key for explaining dynamic issue ownership evaluations. Finally, Lanz and Sciarini (2016) investigate how changing competence evaluations affect party preference. On the aggregate level, they observe stable ownership scores. However, on the voter level, many change their assessments of the most competent party in the course of the election campaign. A more detailed analysis shows that such changes foster party conversion. Voters who change the competence evaluation have a 0.1 to 0.2 higher probability to change their party preference.

Following a general trend in political behaviour research (see Marsh 2002), some scholars have reflected on the *moderating effect of the political context on issue ownership voting*. Green and Hobolt (2008) examine how the depolarization of the British party system between 1987 and 2005 led to increasing levels of issue ownership voting. They argue that in years with low polarization, the campaigns are primarily fought over valence issues. In these elections, issue ownership voting is more frequent than proximity voting. If polarization is high, on the other hand, campaigns are dominated by positional issues, which increases the role of proximity voting and dampens issue ownership voting (see also Green 2007: 630). Lachat (2011) exploits the contextual variation between Swiss Cantons. The study investigates how issue voting varies across different levels of polarization, fragmentation, and proportionality. These concepts describe three dimensions of electoral competitiveness.[13] Lachat argues that voters rely more often on proximity and issue ownership voting[14] in competitive settings. In contrast to Green and Hobolt (2008), the author does not assume a trade-off between issue ownership voting and proximity voting. The empirical analysis bolsters most of the assumptions. However, not all dimensions of electoral competitiveness are equally important: "party system polarization appears to be the single most influential factor" (Lachat 2011: 660). Finally, Pardos-Prado (2012: 344) claims that polarization increases attention on all aspects of political competition, including competence. While it may be difficult to assess proximity in ideologically converged systems, it is not less difficult to evaluate competence. In turn, competence evaluations are more accessible in polarized systems and thus more pivotal for the decision process. This argument gains empirical support; Pardos-Prado (2012) demonstrates a positive relationship between polarization and issue ownership voting.

2.6 CONCLUSION

The classical models of voting put different weights on the role of issues in elections. In the *Columbia model* of voting, issue preferences are closely related to group memberships and have no independent effect on the vote. In the *Michigan model*, issue preferences come only into play when partisanship fails to predict the vote choice. In the *rational choice theory of voting*, policies are the key factor in elections. It advances the image of a voter who seeks to maximize his or her personal benefit by selecting parties that promise a certain policy outcome.

Apart from a few exceptions (Kuechler 1991; RePass 1971), initial issue ownership studies focused on the party level. Budge and Farlie (1983) claimed that parties win elections if their issue is salient during the campaign. They talk past each other and emphasize only issues they own. In a pathbreaking study, Petrocik (1996) revitalized this argument and gave first insights into the micro-level foundations of the issue ownership theory. This thread has been picked up by numerous researchers who mostly found that competence evaluations have a strong and robust effect on electoral preferences (Bellucci 2006; Evans 1999; Nadeau et al. 2001; Sanders et al. 2001).

Over the past decade, several refinements have been introduced to the basic issue ownership model of voting. The distinction between associative and competence ownerships has led to a more careful definition of the issue ownership concept. However, for the voting behaviour literature, the usefulness of associative ownership remains ambiguous. No evidence points to a direct effect of associative issue ownership on the vote. More promising are models postulating an indirect effect (Lachat 2014). Given these results, the competence notion will likely remain "at the heart of the issue ownership theory" (Green and Hobolt 2008: 462).

Another development is with regard to the finding that issue ownership is more volatile than presumed. While the results are mixed in terms of aggregated issue ownership, most studies on the individual level point to high levels of volatility (e.g. Lanz and Sciarini 2016). This, however, raises questions about the determinants of issue ownership.

An important refinement of the issue ownership model of voting concerns the introduction of salience to the model. Some studies include the salience element by combining party competence evaluations with the question on the MIP (e.g. Clarke et al. 2004; Pardos-Prado 2012). Recently, an increasing number of national election studies questions participants about the most competent party on a list of (predefined) issues. The advantage of this method is that competence evaluations are available for the entire electorate. On the flip side, many of these studies have dropped questions on issue salience. While these surveys allow for a finer-grained analysis of how issue-handling competence is evaluated across the entire electorate, we can no longer be sure that these issues are perceived important. Given that issue salience has been found to be a vital moderator of issue ownership voting, this might leave us with underspecified issue ownership voting models.

Until today, issue ownership research is largely focused on single-country studies. Related to this, efforts to explore the moderating effect of the context remain scarce. Some have investigated the conditioning effect of party system polarization on issue ownership voting. While one group of scholars claims that polarization fuels issue ownership voting (Lachat 2011; Pardos-Prado 2012), others argue that polarization dampens the effect of competence evaluations on the vote (Green and Hobolt 2008). However, this literature is still in its infancy. After establishing the basic model of issue ownership voting (chapter 6), this project aims to explore if contextual factors moderate the impact on party competence ratings on the vote choice (chapter 7).

Chapter 3

Theoretical Framework

The president has not yet been able to demonstrate the stability nor some of the competence that he needs to demonstrate in order to be successful.
Bob Corker, Chattanooga, Tennessee, 17 August 2017

This chapter presents the theoretical framework for this study. It is structured along the three research questions. In the first section, I discuss the sources of issue ownership (section 3.1). I then turn to the heart of this study, namely issue ownership voting. This section describes the background for the basic issue ownership voting hypotheses claiming that competence evaluations matter for the vote choice (section 3.2). Section 3.3 discusses how issue ownership voting might be moderated by the political context. This part of the literature is still fairly undertheorized which means that my hypotheses are of more exploratory nature than the ones on the origins and consequences of issue ownership.

3.1 THE SOURCES OF ISSUE OWNERSHIP

Despite being the central element of individual-level issue ownership, only scant research investigated the origins of party competence evaluations (but see De Bruycker and Walgrave 2014; Stubager and Slothuus 2013; Walgrave and De Swert 2007). In fact, we know much less about party competence ratings than about the main concepts of other voting theories. As I have outlined in the previous chapter, issue ownership refers to the link between parties and issues (Walgrave, Tresch, and Lefevere 2015: 778). This book is about competence ownership, which is defined as a voter's perception regarding a party's competence to handle a political issue (Green and Hobolt 2008: 426).

Two strands of research have developed fairly different views on the drivers of issue ownership. According to the first, issue ownership follows a *top-down process*. By shifting the attention from one topic to another, parties can gain or lose ownership. This literature sees issue ownership as a strategic tool that parties can use in their struggle for votes (Meguid 2005). Another way of influencing ownership is through performance. Government parties gain ownership when they perform well and are punished for a bad performance. Opposition parties, on the other hand, gain competence when incumbent parties fail, whereas they suffer from good government performance. A second group of researchers rejects the idea that issue ownership can be manipulated by the actions of political parties. They posit that voters' competence evaluations are mostly an expression of party identification and position (Stubager 2018; van der Brug 2017; Walgrave et al. 2016). In other words, issue ownership is generated in a *bottom-up process* (i.e. derived from voter characteristics). This implies a limited strategic value of issue ownership in party competition.

3.1.1 Issue Emphasis

One of John Petrocik's widely cited claim is that competence ownership comes from a party's or candidate's reputation of handling certain issues. It is "produced by a history of attention, initiative, and innovation toward these problems" (1996: 826). After twenty years, this statement is reflected in the mainstream research, where issue emphasis is considered the single most important determinant of issue ownership (e.g. Budge and Farlie 1983; Green-Pedersen and Mortensen 2015; Meguid 2005; Walgrave and De Swert 2007). For instance, Green-Pedersen and Mortensen (2015) measure historical issue ownership with the attention a party devotes to an issue in its manifesto. They find that issue attention is stable over time and contains party-specific elements. This explains why candidates and parties strategically talk about issues that are beneficial to them and hurt their opponents (Green-Pedersen 2007; Petrocik, Benoit, and Hansen 2003; Sellers 1998; Simon 2002).[1] Nevertheless, the underlying mechanism of issue emphasis is ambiguous. Manifestos can be seen as an expression of issue ownership (i.e. parties emphasize issues they assume to be regarded competent to handle) or as a mean to generate and reinforce issue ownership (i.e. gain ownership in the eyes of the voters). In her article on mainstream party reactions to niche party success, Meguid (2005) is more specific on this point. By measuring changes of issue ownership with changes of issue emphasis, she postulates a top-down version of competence ownership. When altering their manifestos,[2] parties can increase their reputation on certain issues, which makes issue ownership a powerful tool in the parties' "toolkit" (Meguid 2005: 349). This perspective speaks to the idea that issue ownership needs regular reinforcement, preferably during election campaigns (e.g. Petrocik 1996: 828). Most importantly however, it implies that parties have an important say in the issue ownership game. Or, as Budge put it, ownership implies establishing a reputation for greater competence "by emphasising certain topics more than others" (2015: 761).[3]

Thus far, we have only little empirical proof that emphasis actually shapes individual issue ownership. A notable exception is Wagner and Zeglovits, who find that party communication indeed informs competence: "Many respondents appeared to deduce competence from the amount of time a party talks about a topic and how much it advertises these elements of its program" (2014: 288). However, this finding is based on an analysis of twenty cognitive interviews and needs further empirical testing. Based on this discussion, I propose the following hypothesis:

Hypothesis (H)1: The more a party emphasizes an issue in its manifesto, the more likely it is to be evaluated competent in dealing with it.

3.1.2 Performance

Petrocik (1996) distinguishes two types of issues which are linked to different sources of issue ownership. In most cases, ownership is constituency-based (see section 3.1.3). Occasionally, however, ownership is linked to the record of the incumbent party. More specifically, opposition parties gain advantage over an issue if the governing party can be blamed for current complications. When incumbents perform well, they are associated with achieving "good times" (1996: 872) and take over ownership. This form of ownership is limited to so-called "performance issues" (1996: 872), which are conceptually similar to Budge and Farlie's (1983: 48) "issues without fixed effects" (see discussion in section 2.3). While the concept is intuitively intriguing, it remains unclear what exactly constitutes a performance issue. Instead of giving a general definition, Petrocik (as well as Budge and Farlie before him) merely provides a list of different performance issues: "wars, failed international or domestic policies, unemployment and inflation, or official corruption" (1996: 872). In the appendix of his book, he further notes that "performance issues are defined as references to the economy, the conduct of foreign relations, and the functioning of the government" (1996: 847). The second list is both more and less exhaustive than the first. On the one hand, it does not mention 'domestic policies'; on the other hand, it includes the 'functioning of the government' instead of the specific 'official corruption'. The distinction between performance issues and other issues has been described as "not completely obvious" (Christensen, Dahlberg, and Martinsson 2015: 141).

Martinsson (2009: 115) raises the question if such a distinction is reasonable at all. It is furthermore problematic that important theorized mechanisms do not find empirical support. For instance, performance-based issue ownership should be more volatile than other forms of ownership. However, there is little evidence for this assumption. Christensen, Dahlberg, and Martinsson (2015) find similar levels of stability for performance issues and other issues.[4] Nevertheless, they do not rule out performance as the source of ownership. On the contrary, they presume that the record of the incumbent drives issue ownership regardless of the type of issue (see also Bélanger 2003; Bellucci 2006). This relates to work on retrospective voting, i.e. voting based on past events.[5] Fiorina argues that "retrospective voting can occur *on any kind of issue*" (1981: 18, emphasis in original). In my opinion, there is little reason to believe that what holds for retrospective voting should not be true for retrospective competence evaluation. Based on this, I propose the following hypothesis:

H2: The more favourably a voter evaluates the government's performance, the more likely he or she is to rate an incumbent party competent in dealing with the MIP (and the less likely he or she is to rate an opposition party competent on the issue).

Like H1, the performance hypothesis implies that issue ownership is generated in a top-down process. However, the degree to which a party can influence issue ownership is contingent on its incumbency status. Government parties are responsible for their performance. Opposition parties, on the other hand, depend on the failures of incumbent parties.

3.1.3 Constituency and Partisanship

The parties' link to the constituency might be a further source of competence evaluations (Petrocik 1996: 827). Constituency-based ownership leans on the cleavage literature, where parties are viewed as the political expression of religious, linguistic, class, ethnic, or regional conflicts (Klingemann, Hofferbert, and Budge 1994; Lipset and Rokkan 1967). Accordingly, political agendas are aligned with the preferences of their constituencies. The link between political program and voter preferences is recursive. Voters are drawn to parties because they promise to solve issues that are important to them. Parties, on the other hand, focus on certain issues to cater to a specific social group and gain their vote. Thus far, constituency-based ownership has not received much attention. A notable exception is Stubager and Slothuus (2013), who find that people assign issue competence to political parties that are perceived as connected to social groups involved in an issue. Constituency is measured by asking respondents about the party that best represents a certain socioeconomic segment of society. One could object that this captures the perception of the links between parties and constituencies rather than the actual preference for a party based on individual feelings of belonging to a constituency.

Investigating the constituency as a source of issue ownership requires an analysis of the cleavage structure in each country, which is beyond the scope of this contribution. Instead, I propose to link constituency-based ownership with the debate on partisanship-based ownership. In *The American Voter*, Campbell et al. (1960: 24) introduced the "funnel of causality" as a metaphor for the decision-making process. In this view, social divisions influence party identification,[6] which, in turn, shapes issue opinions. That is, partisanship-based ownership is ultimately driven by constituency. This means that constituency-based ownership and partisanship-based ownership are not contradictory. They merely focus on different stages in the funnel of causality.

A vast literature deals with the influence of partisan leaning on issue evaluations. The prime example for this is the Michigan School, where party identification is the principal driver of issue evaluations. However, it would be wrong to see the relationship between partisanship and competence evaluations as deterministic. Party identification merely serves as a "perceptual screen through which the individual tends to see what is favourable to his partisan orientation" (Campbell et al. 1960: 133). Theoretically, this process is based on partisan-motivated reasoning (Goren 2002; Lavine, Johnston, and Steenbergen 2012; Lodge and Taber 2013; Taber and Lodge 2006). Motivated reasoning posits that citizens seek out information that confirms prior beliefs (i.e. a confirmation bias), view evidence consistent with prior opinions as stronger or more effective (i.e. a prior attitude effect), and spend more time arguing and dismissing evidence inconsistent with prior opinions, regardless of objective accuracy (i.e. a disconfirmation bias)" (Druckman, Peterson, and Slothuus 2013: 59). This means that citizens use partisanship as an anchor point from which they evaluate party competence. For instance, they have a harder time to admit that their own party acted incompetently on a specific issue than nonpartisans. Following this argument, the direction of the causal relationship is running from party identification to issue evaluation. This perspective gains support from the observation that partisanship is more enduring over time than core political values (Goren 2005). However, it should be noted that other scholars contested this view as too simple. They argue that, instead of being fixed, partisanship is a moving force influenced by events and opinions (Bartels 2002; Carsey and Layman 2006; Fiorina 1981).

Arguably more than other approaches of issue voting, research on competence-based voting has emphasized that issue preferences might be influenced by partisanship. In one of the first analyses featuring competence assessments of the MIP, RePass (1971: 395) notes that competence perceptions might be

"distorted" by partisanship. To cope with this problem, he proposes to introduce party identification in all models of issue ownership voting.

Following Kuechler (1991), competence assessments are either derived
from cognition (i.e. rational considerations) or affect (i.e. party identification). His main argument is that cognition should produce heterogeneous
competence evaluations, while affect leads to homogeneous competence
assessments. Kuechler's analysis of the 1989 European election study (EES)
shows that only one in four respondents has heterogeneous opinions about
issue-handling competence. However, I do not agree with the notion that
homogeneous evaluations are necessarily distorted by partisanship and
heterogeneous evaluations must be based on cognition. It is possible that
someone with homogeneous competence evaluations does not feel close to
any party. To claim that such evaluations are solely driven by partisanship
contradicts an important body of research as it neglects how partisanship is
conventionally measured (Converse and Pierce 1985). Second, the binary
distinction between cognition and affect does not do justice to the nuanced
debates on the concepts that take place in the field of social psychology (for
an overview, see Forgas 2008). Third, it is problematic to argue that decisions
based on partisanship are a pure expression of affect. The way party identification is understood today, it indeed contains elements of rational reasoning.
In conclusion, it is likely that Kuechler overstates the impact of partisanship on competence evaluations. In a similar analysis, Bélanger and Meguid
(2008: 482) show that only 15 per cent of the voters have homogeneous competence evaluations (on four issues). This number is lower for nonpartisans
(8 per cent) and higher for partisans (21 per cent). Moreover, nonpartisans
are twice as likely to not name a competent party. In a more recent study,
Walgrave et al. (2016) find that 10 per cent of the voters have homogeneous
opinions about issue competence.

Nevertheless, even if we set aside the debate on homogeneous evaluations, empirical evidence suggests that partisanship is a strong predictor
of individual competence perceptions: for instance, Wagner and Zeglovits
(2014: 287–288) show that party identification does, "on occasion" shape
competence evaluations. Stubager and Slothuus (2013) find that partisanship
dominates issue ownership perceptions.[7] Therriault (2015: 933) demonstrates
that, depending on the wording, 73 to 78 per cent of the partisans rate their
own party as competent. In two recent contributions, van der Brug (2017)
and Stubager (2018) argue that competence evaluations are strongly affected
by partisanship. In an experimental study, Walgrave, Lefevere, and Tresch
(2014) further show that party preference moderates to what extent new information has an impact on competence evaluation. The theoretical argument
rests on the idea that party identification shields respondents from incorpo-
rating new information into current evaluations.[8] The results show that the

effect of news messages is reinforced when respondents identify with the party. If voters dislike the party, they are less probable to update their evaluations of competence. I suggest a nuanced interpretation of these results. First, news messages have a positive effect on competence evaluations even when respondents display low levels of party identification.[9] Second, to measure partisanship, respondents are asked about how much they agree with the ideas of the party (on a ten-point scale). This measure rather captures positional agreement with the party than party identification.[10] It is unclear, to what extent this variable is equivalent to standard measures of party identification.

In sum, party identification likely affects competence evaluations. Theoretically, this is in line with the Michigan School, where issue evaluations are influenced by partisanship. Moreover, the link between partisanship has been shown in previous studies. I postulate the following hypothesis:

H3: A voter is more likely to rate a party competent on the MIP if he or she feels close to the party.

3.1.4 Ideological Position

The relationship between issue ownership and positional approaches of voting has always been complicated (Therriault 2015). In the founding studies, competence is conceptualized as fully unrelated to positional considerations. The average voter sees elections as an opportunity to resolve problems. He or she is reluctant to deal with the specifics of a solution and to impose ideological consistency on issues: "The key fact for this voter is not what *policies* candidates promise to pursue, but what *problems* (medical care needs, high taxes) will be resolved" (Petrocik 1996: 830, emphasis in original). Presumably, the clear separation of competence and position is a relic from the valence model of voting (Stokes 1963).

Recently, efforts to understand how position and competence are linked have intensified. The basic claim is that voters consider a party competent because it proposes a certain policy to a problem (van der Brug 2017). "It could well be the case that those who consider the Republicans better able to handle crime than the Democrats prefer harsher sentences for criminals and perceive them as most likely to take those measures" (van der Brug 2004: 213). Further evidence for this view comes from an experimental study. Therriault (2015) divided survey participants into three groups and presented each group a different question about competence. He tested the traditional wording 'would do a better job',[11] a position cue wording ('have better ideas and policies'), and a competence cue wording ('are better qualified'). He finds that regardless of how competence assignments are measured, they are strongly related to the voter's ideological position. In other words, liberal voters see the Democrats as competent to solve important issues and conservative voters usually name the Republican Party when asked about competence.

Stubager and Slothuus (2013) suggest that the link between position and competence might be more complicated. For some issues (i.e. environment, law and order), their analysis shows an effect of issue position on competence assignments. While the magnitude of the effect is only "moderately strong" (2013: 584), it is robust even when introducing other sources of ownership to the model. However, in two cases (i.e. redistribution and taxation), issue position does not affect competence ownership.

Two studies from Belgium and Denmark provide additional evidence for the close relationship between position and competence. Walgrave et al. (2016) argue that issue ownership assessments should be untainted by position. To get an idea about how much this is the case, they report the share of voters who consider a party competent with which they also agree positionally. On average, three quarters of the participants assign competence to a party with positions they like. Lefevere et al. (2017) build on this study and include Denmark as an additional case. Empirically, the authors show that compared to a null model, the percentage of correctly classified cases as either owning or not owning the issue increase, when position is added to the model. However, while statistically significant, this effect is small.

Furthermore, some studies measure competence with questions that explicitly contain positional cues (Lefevere et al. 2017). These cues include "best policy" (Aalberg and Jenssen 2007; Green and Hobolt 2008; Martinsson 2009), "good/bad policy" (Christensen, Dahlberg, and Martinsson 2015), "best ideas" (Brasher 2009), or "best solution" (Lachat 2014). From the experimental studies, teasing out the effects of different wordings, we know that this might substantially strengthen the link between position and competence (Stubager 2018; Therriault 2015; Walgrave et al. 2016). The measurement of party competence in this study does not contain such explicit cues. Nevertheless, I propose the following hypothesis:

H4: The more the ideological voter-party distance increases, the less likely a voter is to rate the party competent on the MIP.

3.2 ISSUE OWNERSHIP VOTING

In the 1970s, political scientists were sceptical about the idea that issue preferences have a great impact on the vote choice. Most contributions in the field were under the impression of *The American Voter*, where the majority of citizens are portrayed as being unfamiliar with important political topics.

Those who can express an opinion are often unable to identify the parties' stands on the issue. In 1971, the first empirical analysis of competence-based voting was published. Although David RePass demonstrated that many voters base their decisions on competence evaluations, he did not address the micro-foundations of the mechanism. To this day, work on issue ownership voting still provides little insight into why voters use their perception of a party's competence to handle an important topic as criterion in the decision-making process. In section 3.2.1, I try to remedy this by arguing that issue owner-ship voting is based on three assumptions. In section 3.2.2, I propose two hypotheses on how partisanship and voter-party proximity moderate issue ownership voting.

3.2.1 The Issue Ownership Voter

Although influenced by the proximity and the valence model, "issue own-ership voting" (Petrocik 1996: 833) or "competence-based voting" (Green 2007: 646) has a distinctive perspective on how voters take decisions. In its essence, the model builds on three assumptions.

First, issue ownership voters *select the party providing them with the high-est utility gains*. Unlike in the proximity model of voting, *utility is derived from having an issue handled by a competent party*, not from having an issue handled in a specific way (Petrocik 1996). In other words, issue owner-ship voting is not based on geometrical representation of issue preferences (Pardos-Prado 2012: 343). This has implications for the way parties interact with each other. In the spatial model, parties compete over policies by tak-ing different positions. In the valence model, they emphasize their fitness to achieve a common political goal. Issue ownership voting, on the other hand, has been described as a "synthesis" of these two models (De Sio and Weber 2014: 871).[12] Parties avoid taking position on all issues. They talk past each other and emphasize only owned issues or issues where they assume suffi-cient potential for ownership. More crucially even, parties convert position issues into valence issues by hiding policy trade-offs. For instance, Social Democrats usually highlight the universal benefits of expanding the welfare state (a shared goal) without mentioning related tax increases. In turn, con-servative parties promote tax cuts (a shared goal) but avoid talking about cuts in social services. "Selective emphasis on only one side of a policy trade-off allows parties to frame issues in valence terms (shared goals for the whole community) that are inherently positional (issues with clearly defined policy alternatives)" (De Sio and Weber 2014: 871). This strategy blurs the lines between position and valence issues. Hence, the binary classification of political topics no longer makes sense. This has already been pointed out in earlier contributions. For instance, James Alt notes that "every issue has, or can have, both valence and position aspects (...) To speak of issues as if they were in some way compelled always to be valence- or position-issues is indeed to confound an empirical matter with an *a priori* classification" (1979: 10, emphasis in original). De Sio and Weber (2014) suggest to place issues on a continuum ranging from 'pure valence issue' to 'pure position issue'. However, empirically, the authors do not observe pure issues of any type. In the twenty-seven member-states of the European Union (EU), voters agree most over matters of abortion;[13] same-sex marriage is the most dividing issue. This means that all issues contain a valence part that is received by the voters and that *they can increase their utility gains by selecting the most competent party, regardless of the issue this evaluation is based on.* This explains why some researchers find that competence ratings impact the vote even when the issue under consideration is highly positional (Bélanger and Meguid 2008; Lanz 2012; Lanz and Sciarini 2016; Lutz and Sciarini 2016; Pardos-Prado 2012).

Second, *utility gains are moderated by issue importance* and highest for the issue at the top of the voter's agenda. Issue importance is a subjective perception of the personal importance attached to a political problem. This element goes back to RePass (1971: 391): "If we wish to know how issues affect behaviour, we must first find out which issues are salient to individual voters." Distinguishing issues based on importance is quite common in public opinion research. The literature usually defines issue importance as the "degree to which a person is passionately concerned about and personally invested in an attitude" (Anand and Krosnick 2003: 8).[14] Research on issue importance has underscored that individuals are more likely to accumulate information on important issues. Many studies have furthermore demonstrated that vote decisions are influenced by attitudes towards issues that are perceived as important to the individual (see e.g. Aldrich and McKelvey 1977; Fournier et al. 2003; Jackson 1975; Krosnick 1988b; Krosnick, Visser, and Harder 2010; Shapiro 1969).[15] Typically for this line of research, Rabinowitz, Prothro, and Jacoby note that "on the individual level, any issue singled out as personally most important plays a substantially greater role for those who so view it than it does for others" (1982: 57). In the issue ownership literature, Bélanger and Meguid (2008) are the first to provide a theoretical framework for linking issue importance and party issue-handling competence. The authors argue that the effect of issue ownership voting should be conditioned by the perceived salience of the issue at stake. Bélanger and Meguid's results corroborate this idea. If an issue is considered unimportant, being perceived as the most competent party pays only little electoral dividends.

Third, *issue-handling competence is a subjective evaluation, which the voter derives from multiple sources*, most importantly party issue attention, party performance, partisanship, and ideological voter-party distance. In section 3.1, I present these sources and discusse how they are related to party competence evaluations.

Based on these assumptions, I define issue ownership voting *as voting based on perceptions of a party's competence to handle an important topic.* To test this mechanism, I propose the following hypothesis:

H5: Rating a party as competent to handle the MIP increases the probability to support this party at the ballot box.

From a cognitive perspective, this type of voting is less demanding than other forms of issue voting (Lachat 2011: 646). In spatial approaches, knowledge about political issues and the parties' positions on them is key. While some studies have shown that voters are capable of distinguishing different party positions (e.g. Krosnick 1988b), many have found that the public is not well informed about politics (Bartels 1996; Carpini and Keeter 1991; Kinder and Sears 1985; Page and Shapiro 1992). Issue ownership scholars, on the other hand, do not have to share Downs's optimism regarding the *political sophistication* of the average citizen. Petrocik views the voter as ill-informed and, to large extent, indifferent towards the political world. She is reluctant to "impose thematic or ideological consistency on issues, and inclined to view elections as choices about collective goods and resolving problems, and not about the specifics of the resolution" (1996: 830). This makes the voter highly receptive to priming and framing (Iyengar 1990; Iyengar and Kinder 1987; Krosnick and Brannon 1993; Krosnick and Kinder 1990). The cognitive requirement is further relaxed by the assumption that the impact of competence considerations is moderated by the salience of an issue. Other research has shown that voters are motivated to seek further information if they perceive an issue important. As a result of this, they are well informed about the political offer (Holbrook et al. 2005). In issue ownership, voters merely have to see differences in the capability of parties to fix an important problem. This is reminiscent of single-issue voting (Conover, Gray, and Coombs 1982), which Lau and Redlawsk (2006: 12) called a "fast and frugal" decision-making strategy. Lachat (2011: 647) argues that, in terms of the cognitive requirements, voting based on perceptions of party competence on the most pressing issue takes an intermediate position between proximity voting and partisanship voting.

3.2.2 Partisanship and Position as Moderators of Issue Ownership Voting

Spatial models and the sociopsychological model have developed fairly independently of each other. Over the past years however, several scholars have fruitfully connected both approaches (e.g. Adams 2001; Adams, Merrill, and Grofman 2005). For instance, Erikson and Romero (1990) demonstrate that the proximity model of voting is more likely to locate a candidate equilibrium if it contains information on partisanship. Most unified models proclaim additive effects, meaning that issue considerations and behavioural variables have an independent effect on the vote. Lachat (2015) advances a more refined argument. He shows that partisanship decreases the impact of voter-party distance in the electoral process. I anticipate a similar moderating effect in competence-based voting:

H6: Nonpartisans are more likely to base their vote choice on competence evaluations than partisans.

Why should we expect this outcome? Vast research has shown that partisanship is an important shortcut in the decision-making process (e.g. Lau and Redlawsk 2001). Such shortcuts, or heuristics, allow taking decisions at minimal cognitive costs (Chaiken 1980; Eagly and Chaiken 1993). Issue voting, on the other hand, requires a more systematic and costly processing of information. For partisans, issue-handling competence should be less important because they can rely on the low-cost partisan heuristic.[16] In the case of nonpartisans, on the other hand, this heuristic is, per definition, not available. They have to rely on costlier decision-making strategies such as issue preferences. This should result in a high usage of competence evaluations in the voting process.

The situation is different when it comes to the interplay between voter-party distance and competence. Proximity voting is cognitively more demanding than competence-based voting (see section 3.2.1). Hence, we would not expect voters to rely on ideological proximity instead of competence since this increases the costs of voting. Nevertheless, other reasons speak for a moderation effect. Let us consider the example of voter i and party j. The proximity model of voting suggests that i has a high probability to support j if they are close to each other in the political space. In this case, competence is unlikely to boost the probability of casting the ballot for j. Put differently, i's utility is already high from electing a positionally close party. The increase in utility derived from having the most important problem handled by a competent party is marginal. Consider now a scenario where i and j do not share the same position in the ideological space. Voter i gains little utility from electing j. However, if i thinks that j is best at handling the MIP despite its ideological distant position, his or her probability to support the party should be quite high. To test this, I propose the following hypothesis:

H7: Ideologically distant voters are more likely to base their vote choice on competence evaluations than ideologically close voters.

Note that an alternative hypothesis is possible. According to Bélanger and Meguid (2008), a party's issue-handling competence should not be important if the voter does not agree with the party's position on the issue. At this point, it is important to underline that I am looking at the ideological distance and not the distance on the voters's MIP. Ideology, as measured by the position on the left-right axis, summarizes various policy positions (Gabel and Huber 2000; Laver and Budge 1992). This implies that even when voter and party are close, they might not have the same position on the MIP. As a consequence, my analysis does not allow me to make any statement on the validity of Bélanger and Meguid's claim.

3.3 ISSUE OWNERSHIP VOTING ACROSS DIFFERENT CONTEXTUAL SETTINGS

Traditionally, electoral research puts most emphasis on individual determinants of the vote. Over the past two decades, scholars have increasingly questioned this narrow perspective and have turned to the role of the context in decision-making (Franklin and Wlezien 2002; Johnson, Shively, and Stein 2002; Marsh 2002). This research is premised on the idea that individuals live in a political, social, or economic environment and that the specificities of this environment shape how they take their decisions. Following Curtice (2002: 165), "We cannot expect to understand elections and electoral behaviour simply by looking at them through the prism of the voter. Rather, we need also to measure the macro-context within which electoral behaviour takes place." This simple but powerful claim is central to understanding why competence-based voting varies across the countries.

In this study, I concentrate on moderating effects of the party system and the government composition. These factors have proven to play a key role in various types of issue voting (Anderson 2000; Dorussen and Taylor 2001; Kroh 2003). Other indicators, such as economic and social structures or norms and habits are beyond the scope of this book. In line with Dalton and Anderson, I presume that contextual settings are exogenous to decision-making in a single national election. "That is, while we know that voters' choices can affect the institutional environment, we presume that in any one election, institutions are defined and recognizable and thus shape voter behavior" (2010: 5). The literature distinguishes direct, indirect, and contingent contextual effects (Anderson 2007). *Direct effects* imply that the environment directly affects political behaviour. For instance, postal voting might increase turnout (Luechinger, Rosinger, and Stutzer 2007). *Indirect effects* are present, when institutions shape a variable which, in turn, affects political behaviour. For example, Kittilson and Anderson (2011) demonstrate that party system polarization and fragmentation decrease the feeling of political efficacy. This again lowers the likelihood to participate in an election. *Contingent effects* are observed when the impact of an individual-level variable on political behaviour is conditioned by the environment. These effects are important in the present study, as I presume that the impact of party competence ratings on the vote choice is conditioned by a third, contextual variable.

While party systems have multiple dimensions, the effective number of parties (fragmentation) and the dispersion of political parties along the left-right axis (polarization)[17] emerge as the most relevant variables for issue voting. In simple terms, fragmentation and polarization reflect the number and the clarity of choices presented to the voter (Dalton and Anderson 2010). I further analyse the clarity of responsibility, which has received a lot of attention from scholars of economic and performance voting. I argue that the concept might be important to individual-level issue ownership, too.

3.3.1 Party System Fragmentation

In a classical study Kuechler (1991) posited that "the more parties that contest an election, the higher the probability that party positions are fairly close objectively and – more importantly – that they are perceived as close if not identical by the voter" (1991: 97). That is, in highly fragmented systems, citizens find it difficult to match their party competence rating with their vote choice. However, the author also suspects that when the attention on an issue is high, positions might transpire, even when the effective number of parties is high. Unfortunately, Kuechler did not test his assumptions empirically. He instead noted that, further analysis would be needed to substantiate his claim.

It took two decades until Lachat (2011) picked up the thread. To him, fragmentation is, along with polarization and proportionality, indicative of electoral competitiveness.[18] As the effective number of political parties increases, elections become more competitive. This should ease proximity voting and competence-based voting.[19] The reason for this is the smaller party size in fragmented systems. That is, a party's electoral base is more homogeneous in terms of its ideological position. Consequently, the impact of issue voting is expected to be strengthened. Even though Lachat's findings do not conclusively support his assumptions, I propose the following hypothesis:

H8a: The higher the level of fragmentation, the higher the impact of party issue competence ratings on the vote choice.

Some research on proximity voting suggests a different view on the relationship between fragmentation and issue voting than the one described in

H8a. Deriving assumptions from this literature is of course tricky, since it presumes that issue ownership voting and proximity voting follow the same dynamics. Given the scant analyses on fragmentation in issue ownership research and their mixed findings, I propose to cautiously borrow from any research interested in the link between fragmentation and issue voting, regardless of the specific type of issue voting.

Kroh (2009) uses the CSES dataset to study proximity voting in thirty countries. He claims that proximity voting is a function of party system complexity. In complex electoral systems, proximity voting is an unlikely voting strategy. Indicators for complexity are polarization, concentration (see van der Eijk 2001), multi-party governments, and fragmentation. In terms of the latter, Kroh (2009) finds that higher effective number of parties ease proximity voting. This yields the following hypothesis:

H8b: The higher the level of fragmentation, the lower the impact of party issue competence ratings on the vote choice.

Hypotheses H8a and H8b are incompatible. For Lachat (2011), fragmentation is an expression of electoral competitiveness. According to Kroh (2009), fragmentation describes party system complexity. What distinguishes the two views is their theoretical focus. Following Lachat, fragmented systems allow parties to express their issues more freely without singling out potential voters (2011: 648). Kroh, on the other hand, concentrates on the voter. The more parties compete on an ideological dimension, the more difficult it becomes for a voter to tell the parties apart and to vote based on voter-party distance. The results confirm his argument: "Proximity is a better predictor if, for instance, the number of competing parties is small" (Kroh 2009: 233).

3.3.2 Party System Polarization

Studies on the interplay between issue ownership voting and polarization are split into two camps. The first posits that the relationship between issue ownership voting and proximity voting is a zero-sum game (Green and Hobolt 2008).[20] If polarization is low (i.e. if parties are ideologically converged), voters can no longer distinguish parties based on positional proximity. As a consequence, they shift to other types of issue voting such as competence-based voting.[21] "We expect competence or valence considerations to be relatively more important to a voter's utility when parties take very similar positions on an issue, whereas we expect proximity to matter more when parties are polarized" (Green and Hobolt 2008: 463). In the case of Great Britain, the authors observe that polarization coincides with increasing levels of proximity voting. In the depolarized party system of 2005, voters rely on issue ownership voting. While party competence proves to be a strong indicator of the vote choice, proximity voting decreases in strength (Green and Hobolt 2008: 470). Theoretically, this mechanism builds on Stokes's distinction between valence and position issues. In depolarized party systems, campaigns are likely to be dominated by valence issues: "Competence should matter more in elections that are primarily fought on valence issues, whilst the spatial model is expected to provide greater explanatory power in elections dominated by position issues" (Green and Hobolt 2008: 462). In other words, polarization causes growing salience of position issues, which, in turn, decreases the impact of competence on the vote (Green 2007: 630). Based on this argument, the relationship between polarization and competence-based voting is as follows:

H9a: The higher the level of polarization, the lower the impact of party issue competence ratings on the vote choice.

A second camp postulates the opposite effect, namely that polarization eases competence-based voting. Pardos-Prado (2012) finds that competence ratings have a stronger effect when parties take ideologically distinct positions. This supports the view that polarization increases attention on all aspects of political competition, including party competence. It might be as difficult to assess a party's competence on an issue in depolarized environments, as it is to assess voter-party distance. In polarized systems on the other hand, competence ratings are more accessible and therefore have a higher impact on electoral decision-making. Pardos-Prado (2012: 344), moreover, does not find evidence for the zero-sum argument. In fact, his results show that competence-based voting goes hand in hand with proximity voting.[22] This is not entirely surprising since the reasoning of the zero-sum camp hinges on a clear distinction between valence and position issues. However, the discussion in section 3.2.1 has shown that this conceptualization might be overly simplistic.

Pardos-Prado's findings are supported by Lachat (2011), who analyses electoral competitiveness of Swiss cantonal party systems and their moderating role on issue ownership voting and proximity voting. Lachat argues that high levels of polarization encourage parties to express their issue priorities and issue positions more clearly. This causes a reinforcement of competence-based voting as well as proximity voting. Lachat does not find evidence for the zero-sum hypothesis either. However, he finds a trade-off between partisanship voting, on one hand, and proximity voting and issue ownership voting, on the other hand. High levels of polarization foster issue ownership voting and proximity voting. Partisanship voting, on the other hand, increases when parties converge on the left-right axis. The considerations of this second camp can be summarized in the following hypothesis:

H9b: The higher the level of polarization, the higher the impact of party issue competence ratings on the vote choice.

3.3.3 Clarity of Responsibility

The concept 'clarity of responsibility' was developed within the economic voting framework. This field of research sees elections as "referenda on the incumbent administration's handling of the economy" (Fiorina 1981: 26). They are opportunities to hold governments accountable for their performance (Key 1966). On the voter level, citizens reward incumbent parties for good performance and punish them for bad performance. In its essence, economic voting follows a simple pattern (Lewis-Beck and Stegmaier 2007: 530): The voter first attributes to the governing party responsibility for handling the economy. The voter then evaluates the state of the economy. Depending on the voter's evaluation, he or she finally penalizes or rewards the incumbent with his or her vote.

Clarity of responsibility is the scholarly answer to the finding that economic voting varies between countries (Lewis-Beck 1988; Paldam 1991). In low-clarity cases, power is shared among several parties. In high-clarity systems, on the other hand, power lies in the hands of a single party (Tillman 2008: 1294). In a pathbreaking study, Powell and Whitten (1993) pointed out that attributing responsibility can be difficult when the institutional and governmental settings are complex. In these systems, citizens are less likely to base their vote on government performance. Over the past years, numerous studies with varying measurements have bolstered this finding (e.g. Anderson 2000; Nadeau, Niemi, and Yoshinaka 2002; Powell 2000). Furthermore, the concept has been fruitfully introduced to other fields of issue voting (Anderson 2006; de Vries, Edwards, and Tillman 2011; Giger 2011; Hobolt, Tilley, and Banducci 2013) and even expanded to political participation (Tillman 2008). I posit that clarity of responsibility can affect issue ownership voting in two ways.

First, H2 presumes that government performance influences how voters attribute issue-handling competence to parties. If the incumbent performs well, citizens will likely rate it as competent, simply for achieving "good times" (Petrocik 1996: 872). In countries where government power is diffuse, voters might find it more difficult to evaluate party competence based on performance. While this does not necessarily influence issue ownership voting *per se*, it certainly means that parties have less means to influence their public image. Second, clarity might also have a direct effect on issue ownership voting. In low-clarity democracies, citizens cannot rely on a policy getting adapted, even when their preferred party is in power. The fact that parties cannot unilaterally implement policies introduces uncertainty to issue ownership voting and likely decreases the role of competence considerations in elections. I thus propose the following hypothesis:

H10: The higher the clarity of responsibility, the higher the impact of party issue competence ratings on the vote choice.

3.4 ALL HYPOTHESES AT A GLANCE

Figure 3.1 gives an overview of the hypotheses. I expect that ideological distance, issue attention, performance, and partisanship shape how voters

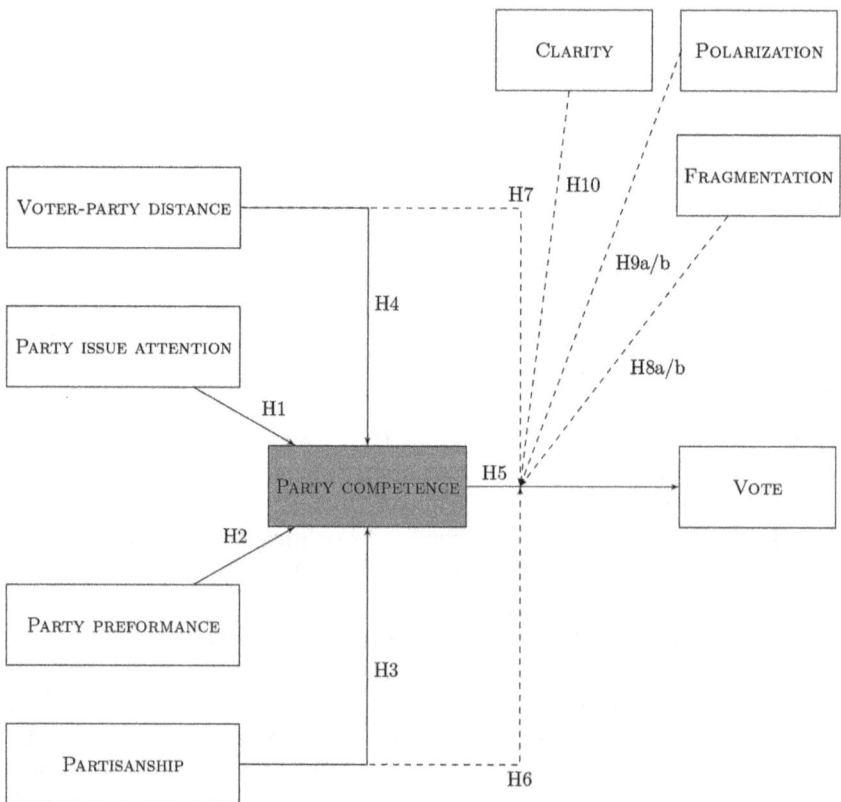

Figure 3.1. Theoretical Framework: Overview

Note: Solid lines depict direct effect; dotted lines are moderating effects.

evaluate a party's issue-handling competence. The respective hypotheses (H1–H4) are tested in chapter 5.

In chapter 6, I tackle the issue ownership voting hypothesis (H5) and analyse how competence-based voting is moderated by partisanship (H6) and voter-party distance (H7). In the chapter 7, I test if issue ownership voting varies across different levels of fragmentation (H8a/b), polarization (H9a/b), and clarity of responsibility (H10). The figure suggests a fairly straightforward sequence of events: based on four pre-existing factors, voters attribute competence to a political party. In a second step, they use this evaluation to decide which party they want to support at the ballot box. However, the schematic presentation is a simplification of the voting process and comes with three important limitations.

First, *the different sources may be related to each other*. For example, in the Michigan model, issues preferences are causally downstream from partisanship. In a similar vein, it is possible that party issue attention affects how voters evaluate a party's position in the ideological space. It is not the aim of this book to show how these concepts are related to each other. However, this implies that partial models testing one hypothesis at the time could easily overestimate the impact of a single source. Due to this, I rely on full models including all sources when testing H1 to H4.[23]

Second, *I do not theorize the relationship between the sources of issue ownership and the vote*. A large body of electoral research has postulated that ideological distance, government performance, and partisanship are key factors in the decision-making process. It is beyond the scope of this analysis to contribute to this literature. However, I control for these factors in all models of the vote choice and report the respective parameters in the regression tables. In general, my findings are in line with the basic assumptions of performance voting, proximity voting, and partisanship voting. A positive evaluation of the government's performance increases the likelihood to vote for incumbent parties. Further, voters are more probable to support a party if they are partisans and if they are ideologically close to the party.

Third and most importantly, in many cases in this analysis I am *not able to demonstrate causal links* between the concepts. The sequence of events is derived from theoretical assumptions, which are, in turn, based on extensive research. Let us, for instance, consider H3. This hypothesis claims that partisanship shapes the way voters evaluate party competence. However, it is possible that causality flows from competence to partisanship. Researches have argued that partisanship is a running tally of political evaluations (e.g. Fiorina 1981). In this line of thought, a party's competence to handle an important problem could be one of factors used to update partisanship. This problem concerns the issue ownership voting hypothesis (H5) too. It might be the case that respondents cast their ballot for a specific party and evaluate competence *ex post*, that is, when they answer the survey question. If this is true, party choice determines competence evaluations, rather than the other way around. It is difficult to assess the magnitude of this problem and, in this particular case, impossible to find an empirical solution to it. Two main arguments speak against an inverse causal effect. First, a large body of research has supported the claim that issue preferences impact the vote choice. Second, the national election studies used in the empirical part ask the question on party issue-handling competence before they enquire about the vote decision.[24] While this does not solve the problem, we can at least presume that survey participants were not additionally primed on their vote decision before answering the question about the party best at handling the MIP. Note that uncertainty about cause and effect is common to most survey-based studies of the vote choice. Experimental data could be a possible way out of this problem. Unfortunately, such data do not exist at this time.

Chapter 4

Empirical Framework

Frau Merkel ist reichlich inkompetent. Sie ist abhängig von ihrer Bürokratie, die ihr diktiert, was zu tun ist und was nicht zu tun ist.[1]
Gerhard Schröder, Interview in *Der Spiegel*, 27 May 1996

Testing the hypotheses imposes high requirements on the case selection and data. The purpose of the following pages is to present the sample of the countries, the various data sources, and the operationalization. As we will see in section 4.1, the main criteria for the case selection are a long history of democratic experience, a high level of economic development, and data availability. Section 4.2 introduces the CSES and discusses how the voter-level variables are measured. The main focus here lies on the operationalization of the key concepts 'party competence' and 'vote choice'. In section 4.3, I present the Comparative Manifestos Project (CMP), the Parliaments and Governments Database (ParlGov), and the Comparative Political Data Set (CPDS). I use these projects to measure party-level and country-level variables such as a party's issue attention, the fragmentation and polarization of the political system, or the clarity of responsibility.

4.1 CASE SELECTION

The sample of countries consists of advanced democracies for which voter-level, party-level, and country-level data are available. The starting point of the case selection is the CSES.[2] This project includes a large number of post-election surveys with questions on the vote choice and party competence. I further restrict the analysis to member countries of the Organisation for Economic Co-operation and Development (OECD). Although Chile, Israel,

Mexico, South Korea, and Turkey meet these requirements, they are excluded since they do not appear in the ParlGov, the CMP, or the CPDS.[3] Furthermore, five members of the OECD are not part of the CSES project (Italy, the UK, Hungary, Belgium, and Luxembourg). In the cases of Italy and the UK, I obtained national post-election surveys containing all important items.[4] Hungary, Belgium, and Luxembourg are not part of the final sample because either no election survey was conducted or the datasets do not contain information on party competence.

The final sample has a heavy concentration of Western European countries (see table 4.1). Additionally, it includes Canada, the United States, plus the Oceanian countries Australia and New Zealand. Clearly, this is only a

Table 4.1. Country Selection

Country	Election	CSES	ParlGov	CMP	CPDS	Included
Australia	2007	✓	✓	✓	✓	✓
Austria	2008	✓	✓	✓	✓	✓
Canada	2008	✓	✓	✓	✓	✓
Chile	2009	✓		✓		
Czech Republic	2010	✓	✓	✓	✓	✓
Denmark	2007	✓	✓	✓	✓	✓
Estonia	2011	✓	✓	✓	✓	✓
Finland	2011	✓	✓	✓	✓	✓
France	2007	✓	✓	✓	✓	✓
Germany	2009	✓	✓	✓	✓	✓
Greece	2009	✓	✓	✓	✓	✓
Iceland	2009	✓	✓	✓	✓	✓
Israel	2006	✓				
Italy	2013	a	✓	✓	✓	✓
Mexico	2009	✓		✓		
Netherlands	2010	✓	✓	✓	✓	✓
New Zealand	2008	✓	✓	✓	✓	✓
Norway	2009	✓	✓	✓	✓	✓
Poland	2007	✓	✓	✓	✓	✓
Portugal	2009	✓	✓	✓	✓	✓
Slovakia	2010	✓	✓	✓	✓	✓
Slovenia	2008	✓	✓	✓	✓	✓
South Korea	2008	✓		✓		
Spain	2008	✓	✓	✓	✓	✓
Sweden	2006	✓	✓	✓	✓	✓
Switzerland	2007	✓	✓	✓	✓	✓
Turkey	2011	✓		✓		
United Kingdom	2010	a	✓	✓	✓	✓
United States	2008	✓	b	✓	✓	✓
		27	24	28	24	24

Note: (a) national election study and (b) my coding.

fraction of all democracies in the world. However, the focus on OECD members means that all countries share several features. First, they score high on economic development and are committed to the market economy. If voters in different countries are concerned about economic issues (and many of them are), it is fair to assume that they live in similar economic systems and often share similar experiences and opportunities. Second, all countries have a long-standing democratic experience, most notably in holding free elections on a regular basis. This transpires from various democracy measurements such as the Freedom House index or Polity IV.[5] For instance, all countries score the maximal value on the political-rights dimension in the Freedom House report since 1999. Third, many of the countries have political parties with long histories. This is important as classic research presumes that ownership is unlikely to change or be built up in the course of few years. Fourth, party competition is structured along the left-right or, in the case of the United States, the conservative-liberal axis. This is crucial when I investigate the connection or the interaction between ideology and issue ownership (H4 and H7). Evidently, this sample comes with a drawback. It does not allow generalizing the findings to other democratic systems. In this sense, the analysis and all its results are restricted to economically developed countries with a long history of free and fair elections.

4.2 VOTER DATA

As in all studies on issue voting, individual-level data have to contain information on the voters' issue preferences and their party choice. Moreover, to analyse the impact of the political system on the decision-making (H8a/b, H9a/b, and H10), contextual variation is key. The present study seeks to achieve this by including a large number of countries. These requirements are met by the CSES,[6] a collaborative research program among election study teams from fifty countries.[7] Participating countries agree to include a common module of public opinion questions in their national post-election studies. The studies are then merged into a single data file. The most recent fourth module does not ask questions on party competence, which is why I employ the third module consisting of election studies from 2006 to 2011.[8]

Table 4.2 lists all individual-level indicators and their respective CSES survey code. Besides the key variables, 'party competence' and 'vote choice', the data include information on the respondent's partisanship, left-right position, and their evaluation of government performance. Moreover, it contains the indicators' political sophistication, age, sex, and education. Note that I further append election surveys from the UK (2010) and from Italy (2013) to the original data file (see section 4.1).[9]

Table 4.2. Voter-Level Variables

Survey code	Variable	Wording/description
Q2a	MIP	What do you think is the most important political problem facing [COUNTRY] today?
Q3a	Party competence	Thinking of the most important political problem facing [COUNTRY]: which [party/presidential candidate] do you think is best in dealing with it?
Q21c, Q21d	Vote choice	Vote choice Lower House (party list or party of district candidate)
Q20a, Q20b	Party identification	Do you usually think of yourself as close to any particular party? Which party do you feel closest to?
Q13	Left-right position	In politics people sometimes talk of left and right. Where would you place yourself on this scale?
Q6	Government performance	Now thinking about the performance of the [government/president] in general, how good or bad a job do you think the [government/president] has done over the past [years since government took office] years? Has [it/he/she] done a very good job? A good job? A bad job? A very bad job?
Q24a, Q24b, Q24c	Political knowledge	Three information items transformed into a scale. The items are country-specific and are of varying difficulty
D1	Age	Age of respondent (in years)
D2	Sex (female)	Gender of the respondent
D3	Education (high)	Education of the respondent

I use the package mice (van Buuren et al., 2016) for R to impute incomplete data (single imputation) on sociodemographic control variables (van Buuren and Groothuis-Oudshoorn 2011). I do not impute values on the variables 'vote choice', 'most important problem', 'party competence', 'left-right position', and 'government performance' since it is possible that this information is not missing at random.

4.2.1 The Most Important Problem

I measure issue salience with the following question: "What do you think is the most important political problem facing [country] today?" This item is usually referred to as the 'most important problem', or MIP. I recode all answers into eight issue categories (social policy, external relations, services, economy, immigration, security, quality of life, and other issues). The various issues at the bottom of figure 4.1 are a nonexhaustive list of the categories in the CSES dataset. The number of these categories varies between 20 (several countries) and 184 (Denmark). Note that my recoding follows previous studies by Giger (2011) and Roller (1998) and is based on the idea that issues are hierarchical networks (Eichhorn 2005: 9). In this perspective, each issue is part of a paramount issue category. For instance, the value-added tax is a subfield of tax issue which, in turn, is part of a country's economic policy. For two reasons, I choose to recode the issues into highly aggregated categories. First, due to the comparative character of this study, the issue categories have to translate to different settings. An overly fine-grained measure might lead to empty categories and threaten the comparability of the issues across my sample. This is especially problematic when I estimate the effect of the MIP in multilevel models. Second, to link the CSES and the CMP, the recoding scheme should be applicable to both datasets. For example, disaggregating the immigration issue would not make much sense, given the limited available codes for this issue in the CMP.

Even though the MIP question is widely used in electoral research, it is the subject of some controversy. Most prominently this critique has been formulated by Christopher Wlezien and Will Jennings (Jennings and Wlezien 2011: 1; Wlezien 2005). Their main concerns centre around the notion of importance and the distinction between the terms 'issue' and 'problem'.

First, the measure might capture what is on people's mind rather than the actual salience of an issue. When asked about the MIP, respondents could think of issue importance in terms of the society as a whole or the importance of an issue for themselves. However, in the context of the CSES, this critique does not seem entirely valid. Prior to the question about the MIP for the country, respondents are asked about the MIP for them personally.[10] By asking two separate questions, the CSES tries to tackle a possible confusion between the two types of importance. Nevertheless, to some extent the salience component of the question remains ambiguous. This is especially problematic when

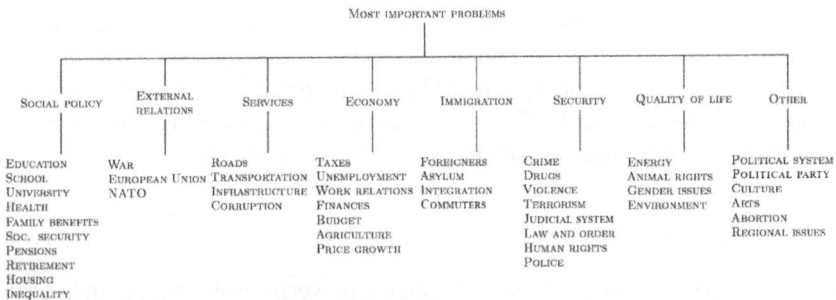

Figure 4.1. Most Important Problem: Coding Scheme

scholars aggregate the MIP variable to measure the broader importance of issues for the society (e.g. Jones 1994; McCombs and Zhu 1995; McCombs and Shaw 1972). Given that I am interested in individual-level effects, a top-of-the-head answer is arguably more relevant than what is important for the entire society.

The second concern regards the distinction between the terms 'problem' and 'issue'. Following Wlezien, MIP confuses the importance of issues with the degree to which they are a problem: "We have reason to belief that the economy is always an important *issue* to voters, but that it is a *problem* only when unemployment and/or inflation are high" (2005: 556, emphasis in original). At this point it is crucial to recall the type of voter issue ownership theory puts forward. Following Petrocik (1996: 830), voters specifically see elections as opportunities to solve problems. Thus, from an issue-ownership perception, enquiring about the MIP (instead of issue), seems appropriate. Moreover, empirically, the distinction between the two terms is not clear-cut. When comparing the survey question on the MIP with a question on the most urgent issue, Jennings and Wlezien (2011: 554) find only little differences: "Issues and problems evidentially are much the same things to people."

Wlezien suggests turning to closed-ended questions (2005: 575). This would also allow respondents to have more than just one important problem. However, answers to closed-ended salience questions might be biased, too: "'It is difficult to tell whether the interview question has elicited merely a fleeting reaction to an issue that is of little or no concern to the respondent, or whether the respondent views it as being truly salient" (RePass 1971: 391). In other words, when presented with a preselected issue battery, respondents might identify issues as important just because they are part of the survey (see also Schuman, Ludwig, and Krosnick 1986). Another danger is that some issues of concern to the respondent might not be included to the question-naire. Consequently, RePass (1971: 65) preferred the MIP measure to the closed-ended measure.

Nevertheless, the MIP question if far from being an ideal measure of issue salience. It distinguishes a single salient issue from all other issues. This means that all non-MIPs are equally (un)important. Such a black-and-white picture is arguably not an adequate description of what goes on in a voter's mind. One solution to overcome this would be to employ relative measures of issue salience where respondents have to rank several issues based on perceived importance. Unfortunately, such measures are not available in the CSES.[11]

4.2.2 Party Competence

Ratings of party competence have become a powerful way of explaining electoral choice. Note that this project is interested in issue-specific competence evaluations and does not analyse competence of politicians (e.g. Mondak

1995) or the general competence of parties (e.g. Green and Jennings 2012b). For reasons of simplicity, I use the term 'party competence' or 'party competence rating' to describe 'issue-specific party competence'. I measure competence with the following question: "Thinking of the most important political problem facing [country]: which party do you think is best in dealing with it?" Issue ownership voting combines the elements salience and competence. Both elements are captured with this operationalization: "The fact that respondents to many national election studies (...) were asked to identify the best party only on the issue they found to be most important reflects the natural connection between these two concepts" (Bélanger and Meguid 2008: 479). From a practical standpoint, intertwining salience and competence reduces the costs of integrating issue ownership to election surveys, which is important for international data projects such as the CSES. However, this measurement strategy has its drawbacks. Most importantly, we do not know which party a voter considers competent on issues that are not his or her top priority. This becomes a problem if competence evaluations are aggregated and referred to as general issue ownership. Consider, for instance, the 2011 Swiss elections. In the post-election survey, 39 per cent of the respondents who considered 'immigration' the MIP named the Swiss People's Party (SVP) as best in dealing with the issue. However, when all respondents had to indicate the party with the best solutions for the immigration issue, only 28 per cent picked the SVP (Lutz 2012: 28–31). This shows that aggregate issue ownership strongly depends on whether we look at the whole electorate or only at the subgroup of voters to whom immigration is the top priority. Nevertheless, for individual-level analyses this is less problematic since they do not expect unimportant issues to impact the decision. On the contrary, combining salience and competence is pivotal for this kind of research (Bélanger and Meguid 2008; Pardos-Prado 2012).

Recently, scholars have started to focus on the question how issue ownership should be measured (Lefevere et al. 2017; Therriault 2015; Wagner and Zeglovits 2014; Walgrave et al. 2016). Wagner and Zeglovits (2014) identify two sources for measurement errors in assessments of party competence.[12] First, respondents might have a different understanding of what the question means. If this is the case, one cannot be sure if observed variation stems from different opinions or the different understanding of the question. Wagner and Zeglovits conclude that the comprehension of the various concepts of competence is fairly good. This includes not only the CSES wording 'best at handling' but also other formulations such as 'competent', 'did the best job', 'will do the best job'. However, a small number of respondents interpreted the best-at-handling question in terms of position or salience. Second, once the respondents understand the question, they have to reach a judgement on the competence of a party. To do so, they need sufficient knowledge and well-formed attitudes. Generally, respondents found it difficult to evaluate party competence. In some cases, this is problematic because respondents provided an answer, despite their admittance to know little about party competence on certain issues. Wagner and Zeglovits (2014: 287) report that only in few cases voters are able to justify their selection with a specific event or an action a party took. Many respondents explained their choice with news reports on parties. The difficulty to answer moreover varied between issues. One could argue that this finding speaks for the combination of MIP and competence. Since respondents first select the MIP, they are likely to be informed and should have less difficulty in assessing the competence on this issue. However, the requirements for evaluating issue-handling competence should not be underestimated.

The variable 'competence' has one category for each party in the country. I assign parties with less than twenty supporters in the survey to a residual category, which I then exclude from all empirical analyses. This decreases the number of respondents from 31,731 to 29,767. Due to missing values on important variables, this number drops by another 4,496 observations (to 25,271). Table 4.3 reports the final number of respondents included in the

Table 4.3. Number of Observations and Parties

Country	Year	N	Parties
Australia	2007	1,672	NPA; AG; ALP; LPA
Austria	2008	686	FPÖ; SPÖ; ÖVP; Grüne; BZÖ
Canada	2008	1,360	NDP; LP; BQ; CPC; GPC
Czech Republic	2010	790	TOP09; VV; CSSD; ODS; KSCM
Denmark	2007	998	RV; KF; DF; V; Sd; SF
Estonia	2011	522	ERe; EK; SDE; IRL
Finland	2011	956	KESK; Ps; SSDP; RKP-SFP; VIHR; KOK; VAS
France	2007	1,344	UMP; PCF; V; MoDem; PS;
Germany	2009	1,404	FDP; SPD; Grüne; CDU/CSU; Linke
Greece	2009	493	ND; KKE; PASOK
Iceland	2009	786	Graen; Ff; Sam; Sj; F
Italy	2013	844	IPdL; PD; M5S; SceCi
Netherlands	2010	1,585	CDA; D66; SP; PvdA; GL; CU; VVD; PVV
New Zealand	2008	707	LP; NZFP; NP; Greens
Norway	2009	1,396	SV; DNA; FrP; V; Sp; H; KrF
Poland	2007	1,091	LiD; PO; PiS; PSL
Portugal	2009	592	CDS/PP; BE; PS; PSD; CDU
Slovakia	2010	698	SDKU-DS; Smer; KDH; SaS; MH
Slovenia	2008	454	SLS; SDS; Zares; SD
Spain	2008	842	PP; PSOE
Sweden	2006	625	Kd; MSP; Vp; FP; SAP; MP; C
Switzerland	2007	1,833	FDP; SP; Grüne; CVP; SVP
United Kingdom	2010	1,975	Con; SNP; LD; Lab
United States	2008	1,618	Dem; GOP
Total		25,271	

Source: CSES, my calculations.

empirical analyses. It, moreover, lists the parties (i.e. the categories of the variable 'vote choice' and 'competence').

4.2.3 Vote Choice

Vote choice reports which party the respondent supported in the Lower House election. In Australia, Canada, and France, vote choice is the party of the elected district candidate. In countries where citizens can vote for party lists as well as candidates (Germany, New Zealand, and Estonia), the variable indicates the party list vote. An exception is the United States, where vote choice reflects the party of the elected presidential candidate. Two main reasons speak for including the United States despite this caveat. First, the presidential elections were held at the same day as the elections for the US House of Representatives. Second, the two parties (Republican Party and Democratic Party) competing for the presidency were, in most states, also competing in the congressional elections. In all post-election surveys, the vote-choice question is only put to respondents who participated in the election.

The original CSES data file contains a category 'other parties'. I additionally assign small parties to the residual category when the number of supporters in an election survey is less than twenty. The residual category is then excluded from the analysis. Table 4.4 gives an overview over the share of respondents in this category before (column 3) and after (column 4) my own

Table 4.4. Vote Choice: Residual Category and Represented Voters

Country	Total No.	CSES (%)	Own (%)	Rep. (%)
Australia	1,764	4	4	93
Austria	885	1	2	94
Canada	2,844	1	1	99
Czech Republic	1,147	3	13	81
Denmark	1,371	0	8	94
Estonia	722	4	11	90
Finland	1,021	2	6	94
France	1,479	4	13	82
Germany	1,526	1	3	94
Greece	740	1	13	85
Iceland	1,260	3	3	92
Italy	950	5	6	81
Netherlands	1,951	0	3	96
New Zealand	1,064	2	10	90
Norway	1,548	0	2	97
Poland	1,213	1	3	96
Portugal	757	1	1	94

(Continued)

Table 4.4. (Continued)

Country	Total No.	CSES (%)	Own (%)	Rep. (%)
Slovakia	874	2	11	79
Slovenia	568	1	22	74
Spain	826	1	13	84
Sweden	1,329	3	5	94
Switzerland	2,037	3	7	88
United Kingdom	2,280	0	6	90
United States	1,564	2	2	96
Total	31,731	2	6	90

Note: Columns 3 and 4: share of voters in 'other party'. Rep. = vote share represented by the parties in the analysis (own coding).

Source: CSES, own calculations.

recoding. In total, 31,731 survey participants from twenty-four countries have voted in their national election. In the original coding, 2 per cent (568) of the respondents fall in the category 'other party'. After my recoding, the size of the residual category increased to 1,964 (6 per cent of the voters). In four countries, the increase of the residual category exceeds 10 percentage points.

An outlier is Slovenia, where 22 per cent of the voters selected a residual party (1 per cent before recoding). Column 5 indicates the vote share represented by the parties in the final variable. In Canada, only 1 per cent of the vote shares are lost in the category 'other party'. In Slovenia, on the other hand, the vote-choice variable only reflects seventy-four of the vote shares for the Lower House. On average, my coding scheme represents 90 per cent of the vote shares. Note that the final number of respondents in the analysis decreases due to missing values on important variables such as the MIP, party competence, or the left-right position (see table 4.3).

4.2.4 Partisanship, Voter-Party Distance, and Party Performance

Party identification is at the heart of the sociopsychological approach of voting.[13] From a theoretical standpoint, these loyalties constitute a psychological affinity to a political party. While partisanship is originally defined as a long-term attachment to a party, the stability paradigm was relaxed over the past years (see Converse 1969; Jennings 2007; Jennings and Niemi 1981; Miller and Shanks 1996). More specifically, partisanship consists of two components, 'direction' and 'intensity' (Campbell et al. 1986). Especially intensity needs regular reinforcement through experiences in the political system. If this is not the case, partisanship might fade. According to Campbell et al., partisanship acts as a "perceptual screen" (1960: 133). This is an important claim since it might impact how respondents assign party competence with "little information and without expending much effort" (Rahn, Krosnick, and Breuning 1994). In the analysis, party identification is measured with the following standard question: "Do you usually think of yourself as close to any particular party?" If the respondent affirms, he or she has to indicate the name of the party. The binary nature of this measure means that no distinction can be made between the parties a person does not feel particularly close to. While this might be in line with the traditional understanding of party identification, it surely is a crude way of portraying party loyalties. Unfortunately, the data at hand do not contain alternative measures of partisanship (e.g. party sympathy).

Besides partisanship, *ideological voter-party distance* is the second important political variable. The literature often refers to the left-right scale as super issue, a common dimension on which various policy positions can be summarized (Gabel and Huber 2000; Laver and Budge 1992). Nevertheless, an ideal test of H4 and H7 would involve measuring the voter-party distance on the voter's MIP. Since such detailed information is not available, I rely on left-right scores.[14] Voter-party distance measures the Euclidean ideological distance between voter (i_{pos}) and party (j_{pos}). In the analysis, voter-party proximity is a matrix where voter i's value for party j is $|i_{pos} - j_{pos}|$ For the position of the voter, I use the CSES dataset, where voters position themselves on an 11-point scale ranging from far left (0) to far right (10).[15] Party positions come from the ParlGov dataset, which averages values from four different expert surveys, namely Castels and Mair (1984), Huber and Inglehart (1995), Benoit and Laver (2006), and the Chapel Hill Expert survey from 1999, 2002, to 2006 (e.g. Bakker et al. 2015; Polk et al. 2017). If a party does not appear in any of the studies, its position is imputed by mean values for the party family. Out of the 117 parties in the analysis, this concerns six parties from three countries.[16]

The use of expert surveys to measure party positions has been criticized in the literature. In an overview article, Budge (2000) argues that it is unclear whose position is being judged (party leaders, activists, or voters) and what the criteria for such judgements are. Further the scores might reflect either intentions (e.g. positions in the party manifesto) or actual behaviour (e.g. voting behaviour in parliament). Finally, Budge posits that it is ambiguous what time period the judgements of position are based on. An alternative to expert surveys is to aggregate individual voter evaluations of party positions. Although technically feasible, this strategy has its own disadvantages: First, many parties are not covered by the CSES, which would mean imputing a great number of party positions. Second, answers to party placement questions are notoriously tainted by projection effects leading respondents to overstate their proximity to parties they like and understate their proximity to parties they dislike (e.g. Page and Brody 1972). A study by Swalve, Bräuninger, and Giger (2017) shows that perceptions of party positions dramatically differ between partisans and nonpartisans and that these distortions have increased over the past years. Finally, it is unclear how voter evaluations overcome any of the problems Budge (2000) raised with regard to expert scores.

Questions on the *performance* of the incumbent party have a long tradition in political science research. Initially, they were mostly used as outcome variable in studies on government approval (e.g. Mueller 1973; Neustadt 1960). With the increasing interest in performance voting, performance questions have been increasingly used as explanatory or moderating variables (e.g. Kramer 1971). In the CSES, respondents are asked to reflect on the performance of the government since the last election (or, if the government changed after the last election since it took office). This means that the question assesses general, not issue-specific performance. The survey participants choose if the performance was (1) very bad, (2) bad, (3) good, or (4) very good. The recoded answers range from 0 (bad) to 3 (good). This scale is then reversed for opposition parties (i.e. they get the value 0 if the government performs very good and the value 3 if the government performs poorly).

4.2.5 Sociodemographic Control Variables

All models control for a number of sociodemographic variables. *Sex* is a dummy variable and is 1 if the respondent is female and 0 if the respondent is male. *Age* measures the age of the respondent in years and takes values between 18 and 100. *Education* is quite challenging to measure in a cross-national setting. The original CSES data file distinguishes eight levels of education. I recode the measure into two categories: (1) low education (no education, incomplete primary, primary completed, incomplete secondary, or secondary completed) and (2) high education (post-secondary, trade school, university undergraduate degree incomplete, or university undergraduate degree completed). In line with Page and Shapiro (1992), I define *political knowledge*[17] as factual knowledge and not as general awareness (e.g. Zaller 1992: 43). The CSES dataset contains three political information items of varying difficulty. Most questions concern the political system. For instance, Australian participants have to indicate whether it is true that the longest time allowed between two elections of the House of Representatives is four years (correct answer: false). In Portugal, citizens are asked about the correct number of countries in the EU (correct answer: 27).[18] Answers to the political information items are coded as 'correct' or 'incorrect'. Based on this, I create an index of political sophistication ranging from 0 (low knowledge) to 1 (high knowledge). The fact that the questions are different in each survey threatens the comparability of the knowledge scores across countries. Differences in observed average political sophistication may stem from actual differences in political knowledge or from varying overall difficulty of the statements. Note that none of the analyses on Slovenia controls for political knowledge, as the information items are not available in this case.

4.3 PARTY AND COUNTRY DATA

To measure a party's incumbency status and its position on the left-right scale, I use the ParlGov database (Döring and Manow 2016).[19] ParlGov contains data on 37 OECD democracies, 910 elections, 1,500 parties, and 1,400 cabinets. I use the same database to approximate the country-level variables polarization and the effective number of parties. Clarity of responsibility is based on the CPDS.[20] This country-level dataset includes information on the political and institutional settings of thirty-six advanced democracies between 1960 and 2015 (Armingeon et al. 2017). Finally, in chapter 5, I investigate how issue emphasis is linked to perception of competence (H1). To perform this analysis, I employ the CMP data, which is based on a content analysis of party programs (Volkens et al. 2017).[21]

4.3.1 Party Issue Emphasis

Party issue emphasis measures the attention a party dedicates to the respondent's MIP. This is done with the CMP where party manifestos are separated into statements (the so-called 'quasi-sentences') which are then hand-coded into fifty-six issue categories. CMP provides the percentage of the statements in a certain policy domain. For my analysis, I first recode the original topics into the same eight issue categories used for the MIP question (see figure 4.1).[22] This yields the share of a party's manifesto devoted to each issue. In a second step, every respondent gets assigned the parties' attention scores on her MIP. This results in a matrix where voters are listed in the rows and the number of columns equals the number of parties in a country.

The premise of this measurement is not that ordinary citizens learn about a party's core issues by reading its manifesto. I rather assume that it adequately "reflect[s] the relative emphasis parties give to the different messages they wish to transmit to electors" (Klingemann et al. 2006: 116). In this spirit, the CMP has been widely used as indicator for "issue emphasis" (e.g. Klüver and Spoon 2016; Ward et al. 2015).

Over the past years, CMP has been the subject of some controversy. Most of the critique regards its ability to measure party positions. For instance, Benoit, Laver, and Mikhaylov (2009) criticize that CMP does not provide uncertainty measures for position estimates. Lowe et al. (2011) point to the flawed scaling technique used for the left-right position. These concerns are of minor relevance for my research since I do not attempt to measure party positions. In line with the original purpose of the project (Ward et al. 2015), I use the CMP to measure issue emphasis.[23] But still, the CMP is by far not perfect. Laver and Garry (2000) note that the separation of the manifesto into quasi-sentences might be a source of unreliability. How this problem can be solved is unclear since hand-coding entire sentences would "put the analyst at the mercy of the writing style of the manifest" (Laver and Garry 2000: 624) and coding individual words without context does not seem feasible either. A further point of critique is the rigid coding scheme. As Ruedin (2013) and Akkerman, de Lange, and Rooduijn (2016: 36–37) note, the CMP does not do a particularly good job in measuring the immigration issue. The available codes 'multiculturalism' and 'unprivileged minority groups'[24] may confound immigration with other political issues. My project is partly able to sidestep this critique since immigration was not a particularly salient issue in most countries. At the time the interviews were conducted, only 6 per cent of the voters considered immigration the top priority.[25]

4.3.2 Fragmentation, Polarization, and Clarity of Responsibility

Party system fragmentation measures the "number of options" a voter can choose from (Dalton and Anderson 2010: 10). One way to go about measuring this dimension of party systems is to simply count the parties competing in the election. This would, however, be problematic, since many of these parties have little chance of winning a seat in the legislature. Laakso and Taagepera (1979) account for this by weighting the parties according to their electoral size so that large parties count more than small parties. This measure is called the "effective number of parties" and takes the following form (equation 4.1):

$$\text{Nr. Parties} = \frac{1}{\sum_{i=1}^{J} f_i^2}, \tag{4.1}$$

where the denominator of the fraction is the sum of the squared vote shares (f) of each party.

Polarization describes the "clarity of choices" presented to the voter (Dalton and Anderson 2010: 14). To that end, it measures how the parties in a country are distributed along important political dimensions. Polarization is low when the parties jointly occupy the same space. If the parties are ideologically dispersed, polarization has a high value. In line with most previous research, I estimate party system polarization on the left-right axis (Green 2007; Green and Hobolt 2008; Lachat 2011; Pardos-Prado 2012).[26] According to Dalton (2008: 906), any good measure of party system polarization should weight party positions by their electoral strength as this guarantees that polarization is higher when a large party takes an extreme position than when a small party occupies the same position. I use the polarization measure proposed by Taylor and Herman (1971), which reports the variance statistic of the party's left-right position weighted by their electoral strength (equation 4.2):

$$\text{Polarization} = \sum_{j=1}^{J} f_j \cdot (s_j - \bar{s})^2 , \qquad (4.2)$$

where f_j is the vote share of party j. The vote shares are rescaled to sum to 1. Here s_j is the position of party j on the left-right scale; s_j averages all answers regarding a given party;[27] and $\bar{s}$ is the weighted average position of all parties on the left-right axis, that is (equation 4.3)

$$\bar{s} = \sum_{j=1}^{J} f_j x_j . \qquad (4.3)$$

Clarity of responsibility describes the extent to which citizens can assign responsibility to governing parties. In the original index developed by Powell and Whitten (1993) clarity of responsibility is low if opposition parties control committee chairs, party cohesion is weak, bicameral opposition is strong, the number of incumbent parties is high, and a minority government is in charge (i.e. the government depends on other parties for its policies). In a later contribution, Powell (2000) uses a simplified version of this index where he distinguishes between five conditions of government majority status: (1) minority government, (2) minority government with outside support, (3) majority government negotiated after the election, (4) multiparty pre-election majority government, and (5) single-party majority government. Powell posits that clarity of responsibility increases as one moves from points (1) to (5). Compared to the original index, this measure is a less fine-grained description of a country's political institutions. On the other hand, the simplified version is more likely to be understood by voters (Giger 2011: 73) and, by putting more weight on short-term structures, it is in line with subsequent research postulating a dynamic understanding of clarity of responsibility (see also Anderson 2000; Nadeau, Niemi, and Yoshinaka 2002).

My measure is built on the 'gov_type' variable in the CPDS and distinguishes five types of government: (1) technocratic government, (2) minority government, (3) surplus coalition government, (4) minimal winning coalition government, and (5) single-party majority government. Following this, clarity of responsibility is lowest in technocratic governments and highest in single-party majority governments.

Chapter 5

The Sources of Issue Ownership

We are the party of economic competence.
Gordon Brown, Labour Party conference, Brighton, 27 September 2004

Although evaluations of party competence are pivotal to the issue owner-ship voting, surprisingly little is known about their origins. For instance, it is unclear to what extent parties can shape ownership. While van der Brug (2004) and Walgrave et al. (2016) posit that issue ownership is mostly an expression of partisanship and position, Meguid (2005) argues that parties can influence their reputation on an issue. In the theoretical framework, I propose a nuanced view. In line with Meguid, I expect parties to be regarded competent if they spend above-average attention on an issue (H1). Parties can further increase their issue-handling competence when they perform well in government (H2). I, moreover, expect positive relationships between partisanship and competence (H3) and between voter-party distance and competence (H4).

This analysis is important both from a theoretical and from a practical point of view. Issue ownership is defined as a link between a party and an issue in the voter's mind. As such, it is a unique concept that should not be entirely driven by partisanship or position. Demonstrating that competence evalu-ations are more than these factors, and that they have multiple sources, is central to my argument that there is no substitute for competence in elections. Furthermore, if issue ownership is subject to manipulation, it indeed becomes a powerful tool a party can use in its struggle for votes. This might have important implications on how parties can run successful election campaigns.

The results will show that competence is related to partisanship and voter-party distance. I further find a strong relationship between party performance and competence perceptions. Voters tend to attribute competence to parties that perform well in government. Opposition parties, on the other hand, are more likely to be seen as competent when the incumbent does a poor job. The results are ambiguous with regard to party issue attention. In the majority of countries, parties are rewarded with increasing issue-handling reputation if they dedicate above-average attention to the issue. However, in one-third of the countries, these effects are substantially weak. In another third of the cases, I find no credible or even slightly negative effects of party issue attention.

5.1 METHOD

To test the hypotheses, I employ voter-level data from the CSES. Party issue attention is measured with the CMP. The incumbency status and the ideological position of the parties are derived from the ParlGov. Detailed information on the data projects as well as the different indicators is provided in the methodology chapter (sections 4.2 and 4.3).

The categories of the outcome variable 'most competent party' cannot be ordered in a sensible way. Variables of this type are usually referred to as nominal variables.[1] In social sciences, the most common statistical models for nominal outcomes with more than two categories are the multinomial logit model (MNLM) and the conditional logit model (CLM) (Alvarez and Nagler 1998; Long 1997; Long and Freese 2001; McFadden 1974). Both models are based on the random utility theory, where functions are estimated to describe a decision maker's gain from selecting one alternative over the other. Let U_{ij} be the utility of individual i when selecting alternative $j = 1, \ldots, J$. Under the assumption of utility maximization, i chooses the alternative giving his or her the highest utility. That is, j is selected, if $U_{ij} > U_{ik}$, $\forall k \neq j$. Since we cannot observe this utility directly, a function containing a systematic component (V_{ij}) and a stochastic component (ϵ_{ij}) is specified (equation 5.1):

$$U_{ij} = V_{ij} + \epsilon_{ij}.$$ (5.1)

In MNLM and CLM, the stochastic component follows a type I extreme value distribution with the density $p\,(\epsilon_{ij}) = \exp[-\epsilon_{ij} - \exp(\epsilon_{ij})]$. This regards all decision makers i and choice alternatives j. Furthermore, ϵ_{ij} is assumed to be independent across alternatives. In other words, the disturbance of one alternative must not contain information about the disturbance of another alternative (Jackman 2009).

I distinguish between two types of variables. The first type varies across decision makers but is constant over alternatives (x_i). Examples are the citizen's age, gender, education, or political sophistication. The second type varies across decision maker and alternatives (x_{ij}) or only across alternatives (x_i). Examples include all sources of issue ownership, that is, a party's issue emphasis, its performance in government, a voter's attachment to a party or his or her positional proximity to the party. While MNLMs use covariates of the first type, CLMs take choice-specific variables.[2]

Both models are too rigid for the purpose of this project. Estimating either pure MNLM or pure CLM implies that the decision is shaped by only one variable type. The result would be a poorly specified model of the vote choice. To avoid this, I run "hybrid models" (Jackman 2009: 418), which use regressors that vary across voters and are constant across alternatives *and* regressors that vary over choice alternative and voters. The systematic component of the hybrid model is specified as follows (equation 5.2):

$$V_{ij} = x_i \beta_j + z_{ij} \gamma , \qquad (5.2)$$

where x_i is a vector with voter-specific predictors and z_{ij} summarizes the choice-specific predictors. Variables of the former type pick up a number of $J\beta$ parameters and choice-specific variables pick up one γ parameter. In this model, the probability of voter i to choose alternative j is (equation 5.3)

$$\pi_{ij} = \Pr\left(y_i = j\right) = \frac{\exp\left(V_{ij}\right)}{\sum_{j=1}^{J}\exp\left(V_{ij}\right)} . \qquad (5.3)$$

Let us now turn to the regression models used to test the four hypotheses (H1–H4). I estimate separate models in each country where the main predictors of party competence evaluation vary across alternatives.[3] The controls are voter-specific and constant over alternatives. This model is specified as follows (equation 5.4):

$$\begin{aligned} V_{ij} = \beta_{0j} + \beta_{1j} \cdot age_i + \beta_{2j} \cdot sex_i + \beta_{3j} \cdot education_i \\ + \gamma_1 \cdot emphasis_{ij} + \gamma_2 \cdot performance_{ij} + \gamma_3 \cdot partisan_{ij} + \gamma_4 \cdot position_{ij} \end{aligned}, \qquad (5.4)$$

where β_{0j} is the intercept for party j. The four sources of issue ownership take the form of a matrix with j columns. Here emphasis$_{ij}$ is the share of the party manifesto dedicated to the voters' most pressing problem (MIP) and performance$_{ij}$ is the government performance and ranges from 0 (bad performance) to 3 (good performance). The scale is reversed for opposition parties. In a country with an incumbent party j and an opposition party k where voter i evaluated the government performance as 'good', cell a_{ij} is 2 and cell a_{ik} is 1. Here partisan$_{ij}$ is the party identification; position$_{ij}$ measures the distance between voter i and party j; and age$_i$, sex$_i$, and education$_i$ are voter-specific covariates.

The most straightforward way to estimate such complex models is in a Bayesian framework. I specify diffuse $N(0,10^2)$ priors for γ and β. Overall, the chains in the empirical part of this chapter are well behaved. High auto-correlation is an issue and leads to low effective sample sizes. While this is not a problem for simulation consistency (Jackman 2009: 192), the runtime of the chains has to be fairly high. I run 150,000 iterations (it.) after a burn-in of 50,000 it. in each model.

Because voter-specific variables produce J parameters, presenting the full regression tables is challenging. To ease the readability, I only show the key parameters (all of which are choice-specific). Since logistic regression parameters are hard to grasp, I rely on graphical presentation of predicted probabilities and changes of predicted probabilities. In both cases, I follow the observed-value approach (e.g. Gelman and Hill 2007; Hanmer and Ozan Kalkan 2013). *Predicted probabilities* are estimated in four steps: (1) I run the model and store the draws of the Markov chain Monte Carlo (MCMC). This yields a matrix with 150,000 sampled values for each γ and β parameter. (2) I multiply the sampled parameters with the observed values (x_i and z_{ij}) of each survey participant. The exception is the variable of interest (i.e. one of the sources of competence evaluations), which is allowed to vary across a range of interesting values. (3) In a next step, I multiply the values set for x_i and z_{ij} with the 150,000 sampled parameters from the MCMC output. (4) I transform the predictions from the third step into predicted probabilities and calculate the median value (equation 5.3). (5) I average these values across all voters in the survey. This is the value I later refer to as the predicted probability. To find the 95 per cent highest probability density (HPD) regions, I estimate the (averaged) 2.5th and 97.5th percentile of the sampled predicted probabilities. I only calculate predicted probability for the observed outcome value. That is, I predict the probability of the actual choice made by a survey participant, given his or her observed profile (except on the variable of interest).[4]

First differences (FDs), or differences in predicted probabilities, show how much the probability of an outcome increases or decreases as a function of changing an input variable.[5] For instance, we might wonder how much a voter's probability of rating party j as best to handle the MIP increases if he or she is a partisan of j. To this end, I multiply the sampled parameter with a scenario 'partisanship' and a scenario 'no-partisanship'. I then subtract the 150,000 predictions (per voter) of the two scenarios from each other. The median of this distribution is what I call the FD; the 2.5th and 97.5th percentiles of the distribution indicate 95 per cent HPD. In a last step, I average these predictions across all voters. The direction of the effect (positive or negative) is highly credible if the HPD of the resulting value does not include the 0.

5.2 ISSUE EMPHASIS

Table 5.1 summarizes the marginal posterior densities of the four γ predictors (see equation 5.4).[6] Each country is represented by two rows. The top rows show the posterior means, the second row contains HPDs of the parameters. This interval spans 95 per cent of the distribution "such that every point inside the interval has a higher credibility than any point outside the interval" (Kruschke 2014: 87). The direction of an effect is credible if the HPD does not contain the value zero ($0 \notin \text{HPD}$).

Table 5.1. Sources of Competence

Country	Emph., γ_1	Perf., γ_2	Pl, γ_3	Dist., γ_4	Cont.
Australia	0.06	0.64	1.59	−0.20	✓
	[0.05, 0.07]	[0.51, 0.78]	[1.43, 1.75]	[−0.26, −0.15]	
Austria	0.20	0.14	2.89	−0.14	✓
	[0.14, 0.25]	[−0.05, 0.33]	[2.58, 3.20]	[−0.24, −0.05]	
Canada	0.05	0.88	2.31	−0.14	✓
	[0.03, 0.07]	[0.70, 1.07]	[2.11, 2.51]	[−0.20, −0.07]	
Czech Republic	0.10	0.01	2.76	−0.38	✓
	[0.02, 0.18]	[−0.22, 0.25]	[2.47, 3.08]	[−0.48, −0.28]	
Denmark	0.02	0.34	2.14	−0.23	✓
	[0.01, 0.03]	[0.17, 0.52]	[1.98, 2.31]	[−0.28, −0.17]	
Estonia	−0.02	0.25	2.79	−0.12	✓
	[−0.09, 0.05]	[0.02, 0.49]	[2.44, 3.17]	[−0.22, −0.02]	
Finland	0.01	0.45	2.93	−0.21	✓
	[0.00, 0.01]	[0.29, 0.62]	[2.70, 3.18]	[−0.30, −0.13]	
France	0.14	0.33	1.79	−0.33	✓
	[0.10, 0.17]	[0.17, 0.49]	[1.56, 2.04]	[−0.41, −0.24]	
Germany	0.05	0.51	2.74	−0.41	✓
	[0.03, 0.07]	[0.35, 0.68]	[2.52, 2.98]	[−0.50, −0.32]	
Greece	−0.03	0.42	3.61	−0.36	✓
	[−0.10, 0.04]	[0.12, 0.75]	[2.83, 4.54]	[−0.58, −0.14]	
Iceland	0.02	0.41	2.82	−0.21	✓
	[0.00, 0.04]	[0.23, 0.59]	[2.56, 3.09]	[−0.31, −0.12]	
Italy	0.01		2.73	−0.30	✓
	[−0.02, 0.04]		[2.41, 3.07]	[−0.39, −0.20]	
Netherlands	0.08	0.36	1.48	−0.23	✓
	[0.06, 0.10]	[0.17, 0.56]	[1.33, 1.63]	[−0.27, −0.19]	
New Zealand	0.02	0.90	1.93	−0.13	✓
	[0.00, 0.04]	[0.60, 1.24]	[1.52, 2.38]	[−0.31, 0.05]	
Norway	0.08	0.39	1.72	−0.35	✓
	[0.07, 0.10]	[0.23, 0.55]	[1.53, 1.91]	[−0.40, −0.30]	
Poland	0.04	0.78	2.94	−0.05	✓
	[0.01, 0.08]	[0.55, 1.03]	[2.57, 3.34]	[−0.16, 0.07]	

(Continued)

Table 5.1. (Continued)

Country	Emph., γ_1	Perf., γ_2	PI, γ_3	Dist., γ_4	Cont.
Portugal	−0.01	0.89	2.37	−0.17	✓
	[−0.06, 0.03]	[0.61, 1.20]	[2.00, 2.76]	[−0.28, −0.06]	
Slovakia	−0.01	0.59	3.37	−0.21	✓
	[−0.06, 0.03]	[0.23, 1.02]	[3.03, 3.74]	[−0.36, −0.06]	
Slovenia	0.03	0.58	2.01	−0.29	✓
	[−0.02, 0.08]	[0.26, 0.94]	[1.53, 2.51]	[−0.43, −0.15]	
Spain	−0.24	0.92	2.30	−0.78	✓
	[−0.47, −0.04]	[0.54, 1.32]	[1.60, 3.09]	[−1.06, −0.53]	
Sweden	0.05	0.54	2.85	−0.21	✓
	[0.01, 0.08]	[0.23, 0.89]	[2.54, 3.19]	[−0.29, −0.12]	
Switzerland	0.09	−0.08	2.31	−0.43	✓
	[0.08, 0.10]	[−0.30, 0.12]	[2.09, 2.53]	[−0.49, −0.37]	
United Kingdom	0.01		2.51	−0.09	✓
	[−0.03, 0.04]		[2.32, 2.71]	[−0.16, −0.02]	
United States	0.02	0.27	1.98	−0.16	✓
	[−0.03, 0.06]	[0.15, 0.40]	[1.76, 2.21]	[−0.22, −0.09]	

Note: Marginal posterior densities of γ (equation 5.4). Numbers in brackets are 95 per cent HPD. MCMC with 150,000 it. after 50,000 it. burn-in. Emph. = party issue emphasis, perf. = government performance, PI = party identification, dist. = voter-party distance, cont. = control variables.

Sources: CSES, ParlGov, CMP, and own calculations.

The question how issue emphasis affects competence ratings is very much a question about the power of parties to influence their public image. According to Meguid (2005: 349), issue ownership is a "tool" parties may use when competing for votes. An important implication of this view is, that parties have (at least some) control over their competence ratings. This resonates with other scholars who argue that issue ownership is established by emphasizing one issue more than others (e.g. Budge 2015; Wagner and Zeglovits 2014). I measure issue attention with the share of the party manifesto dedicated to a problem. H1 is supported, if higher attention increases the probability to rate a party competent on the MIP. In this case, γ_1 has a positive sign.

In fifteen countries, issue emphasis has a credible, positive effect on competence. When asked to evaluate issue competence, voters gravitate to parties that emphasize their MIP more than others. In four countries (Italy, Slovenia, the UK, and the United States), we cannot rule out negative effects despite the positive marginal posterior densities.

In Estonia, Greece, Portugal, Slovakia, and Spain, issue emphasis decreases the probability to be regarded competent. In Spain, this effect is credible. Generally, this lends some support for the issue-attention hypothesis (H1). However, while issue attention is positively correlated with competence in the majority of countries, the results do not support a general confirmation of this assumption across all cases.

To investigate the strength of the effects, I turn to the predicted probabilities in figure 5.1. Each panel corresponds to a country. The y axes show the probability to rate the observed party competent on the most pressing problem. The x axes indicate how strongly the parties emphasize the MIP in their manifestos. The values range from below-average emphasis (i.e. mean emphasis -7.5 percentage points) to above-average emphasis (i.e. mean emphasis $+7.5$ percentage points). For the remaining parties, issue emphasis is fixed on the mean value. The panels are ordered based on the strength of the effect. That is, the FD has the highest positive value in Austria and the highest negative value in Spain.

The probabilities in the first part of figure 5.1 show that the effect of issue emphasis on competence ratings is substantial in some countries. If an Austrian party's issue attention is below average, its likelihood to be regarded as best capable of handling the issue is 0.48. The upward slope in the panel shows that emphasizing the MIP pays off in terms of competence rating. When the party spends above-average attention on the problem, the voters' probability to rate this party competent increases to 0.8. Put differently, Austrian voters are likely to rate a party competent, when the issue is prominently featured in its manifesto. As it turns out, Austria is not an outlier. In four countries (Austria, Switzerland, the Netherlands, France, and Czech Republic), the changes in predicted probabilities are 0.18 or higher. In these cases, a 1 percentage point higher issue emphasis increases the probability of a positive competence rating by more than 0.01. In Australia, Slovenia, Canada, Sweden, and Germany, the FDs are less impressive, but still above 0.08 (when we simulate a change in attention from below to above average). In four cases (Denmark, Italy, Iceland, and Poland) the results line up with H1, but the size of the effect is small (FDs <0.05). In these countries, even large shifts of issue attention hardly impact the party's issue-handling reputation. In eight countries, issue attention does not credibly impact competence evaluations. Spain is the sole country where negative effects of issue emphasis are credible (FD -0.11).

H1 argues that issue emphasis yields a positive effect on competence perceptions. My findings support this claim in fifteen out of twenty-four countries. However, even in countries where H1 is supported, parties are hardly able to substantially boost their issue-handling reputation by shifting attention to the voters' MIPs. To argue that issue ownership is a tool in the parties' hands would be an overstatement in most countries.

An important concern is with regard to the direction of the relationship between party issue attention and competence. According to Budge and Farlie (1983), parties highlight issues they already own. This means that issue attention could be the consequence, rather than the origin of competence. To test if this is the case, I separate the group of voters who evaluate a specific

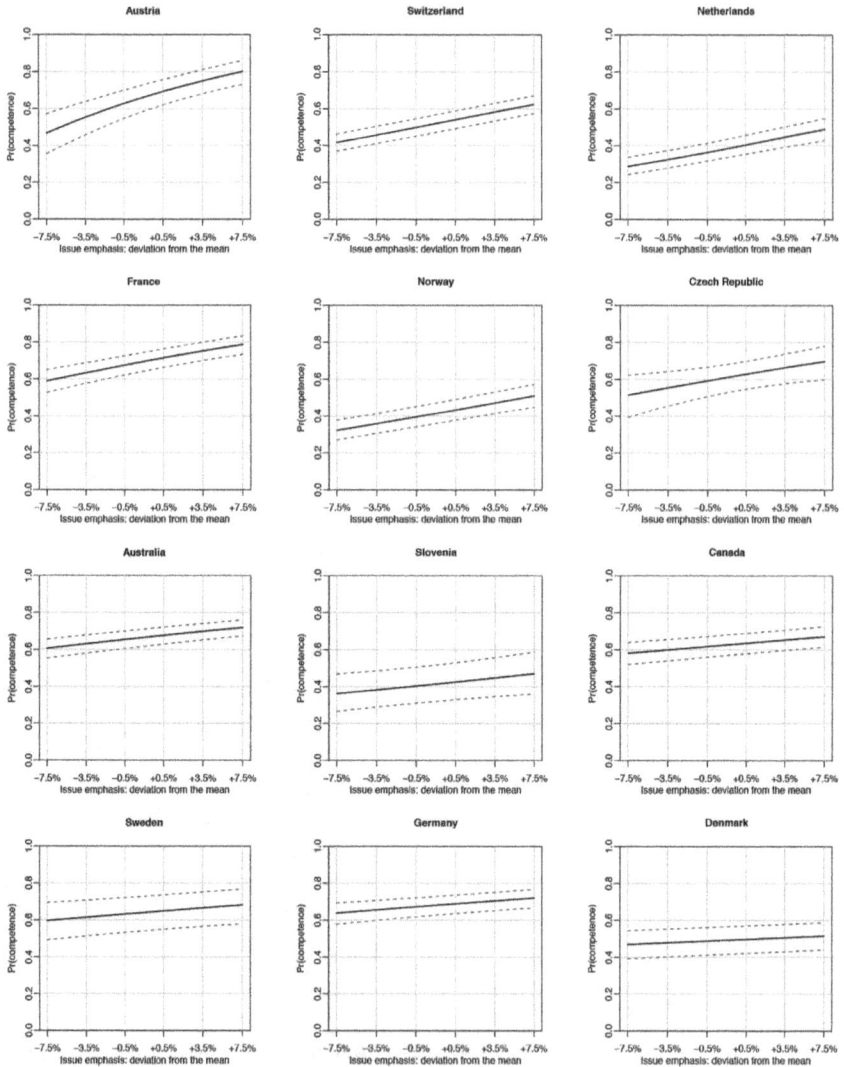

Figure 5.1. Predicted Party Competence and Issue Emphasis.

Note: Effects estimated for the observed outcome. Dotted lines = 95 per cent HPD.

Sources: CSES, ParlGov, CMP, and own illustrations.

party as competent and identify their collective top issue. I then analyse if the party changed its emphasis of this issue after the election. If Budge and Farlie's claim is correct, we should see that parties increase their attention on issues, where they already have a reputation of competence. However, the analysis gives no indication that this is the case (see online appendix).[7] While this does not exclude that parties update their manifestos strategically (Klüver

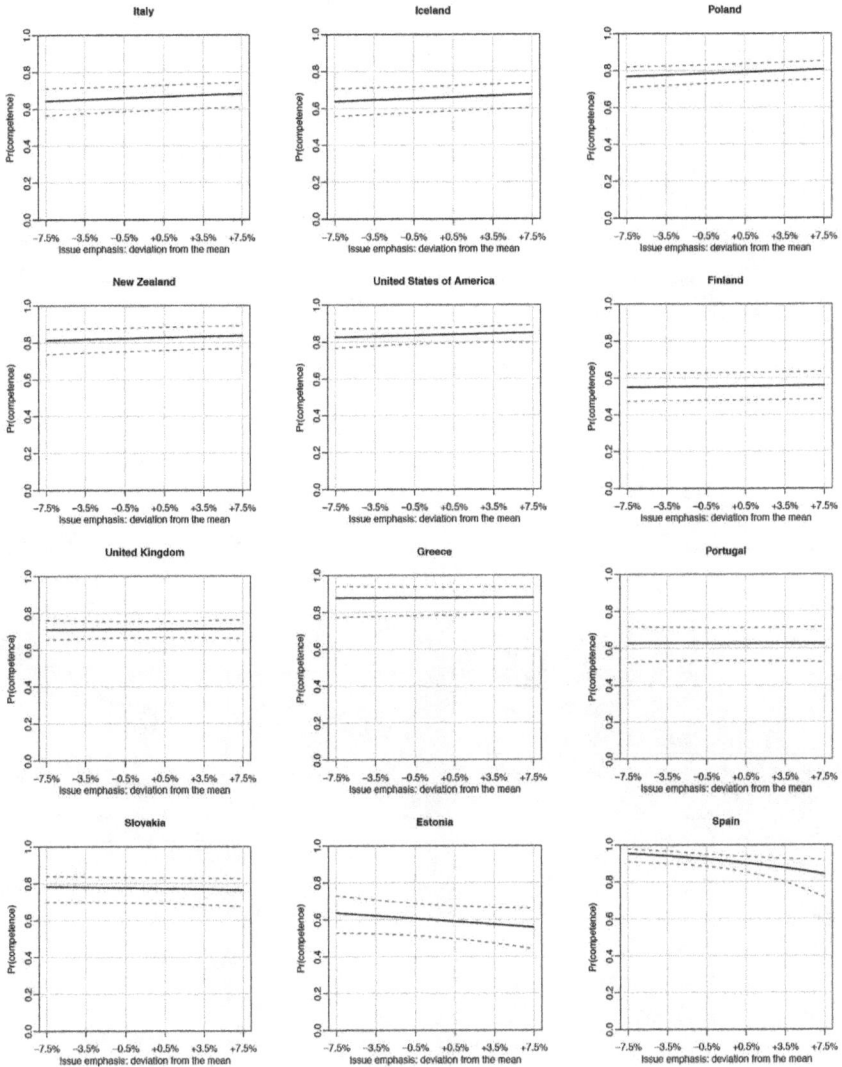

Figure 5.1. (Continued)

and Spoon 2016; Spoon and Klüver 2014), it hints that this strategy does not necessarily involve emphasizing already-owned issues.

5.3 PERFORMANCE

The second source of issue ownership is the performance of the governing party. H2 posits that voters, who evaluate government performance favourably, are likely to rate incumbent parties competent. Opposition parties, on

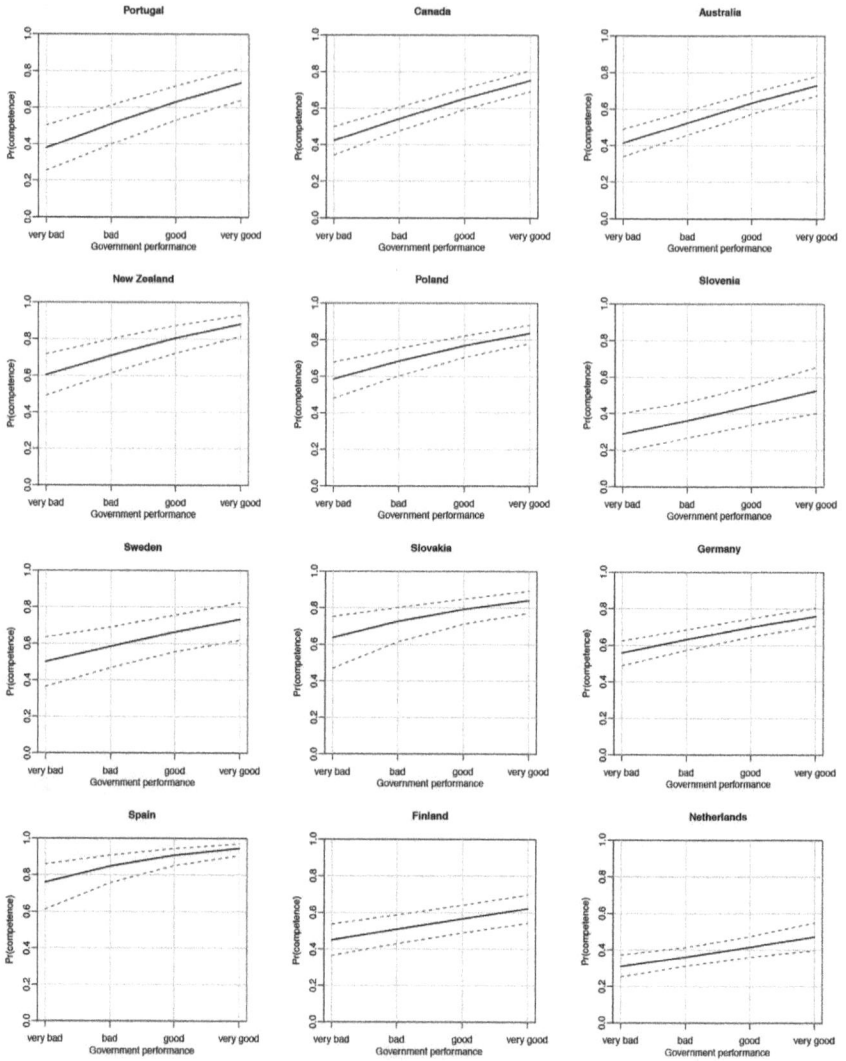

Figure 5.2. Predicted Party Competence and Performance.

Note: Effects estimated for the observed outcome. Dotted lines = 95 per cent HPD.

Sources: CSES, ParlGov, CMP, and own illustrations.

the other hand, gain competence if the government party performs poorly in office. This follows from research on "performance issues" (Petrocik 1996: 872) and issues without "fixed effects" (Budge and Farlie 1983: 48). In line with work on retrospective voting (Fiorina 1981) and previous work on issue ownership (Christensen, Dahlberg, and Martinsson 2015; Martinsson

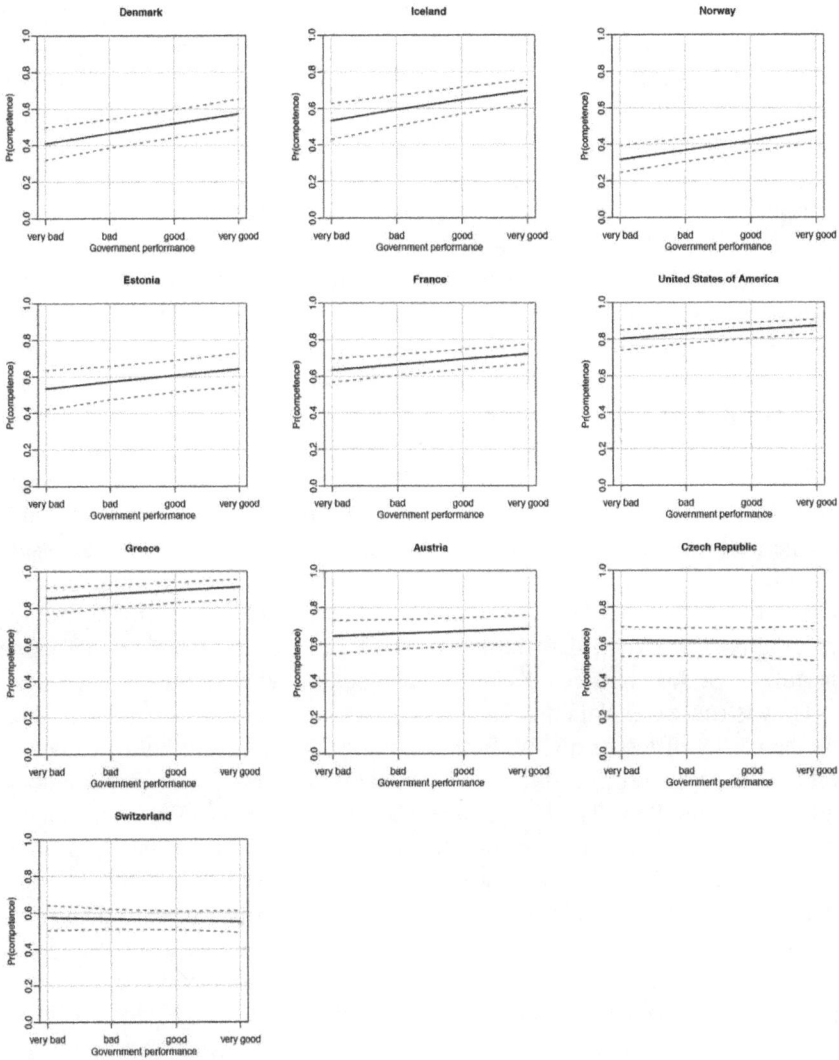

Figure 5.2. (Continued)

2009), I do not expect a moderating effect of different types of issue (i.e. performance issues versus other issues). The basis of the performance measure is a 4-point scale where respondents evaluate how well the government performed. H2 is confirmed, if γ_2 in table 5.1 has a positive sign. That is, performance evaluations are beneficial to the party in question.

The second hypothesis is supported in nineteen out of twenty-two countries. In other words, government performance has an effect on how citizens evaluate issue-handling competence. The predictors in Austria and the Czech Republic have the expected sign, whereas in Switzerland performance yields negative effects for competence. In all three cases, the results are non-credible. Even with these exceptions in mind, there is little ambiguity with regard to the importance of H2.

To assess the strength of these effects, we turn to the predicted probabilities in figure 5.2. The y axes depict the voter's probability to rate a party competent; the x axes show the entire range of government performance (very bad to very good). The order of the panels is again based on the magnitude of the FDs. In many countries, the effects are substantial. In Spain, the FD amounts to over 0.35. In other words, performing well as an incumbent (or being in the opposition when the government performs poorly) takes parties a long way when it comes to competence. Other countries too, see strong effects of performance on individual party competence evaluations. In Canada and Australia, FDs are above 0.3. In New Zealand, Poland, Slovenia, and Sweden, the probabilities to rate a party competent increase between 0.2 and 0.3 as the performance changes from 'very bad' to 'very good'. In nine cases, the FDs are between 0.1 and 0.2. In France, the United States, and Greece, performance does not have a strong impact on the issue-handling reputation of a party. Finally, in Austria, the Czech Republic, and Switzerland, party performance does not credibly impact competence evaluations.

How is can we explain this finding? One answer might be found in research on the clarity of responsibility. In this string of literature, attributing responsibility (and acting on it) is difficult if national institutions diffuse power among different actors (Powell and Whitten 1993). Switzerland has a large government coalition, representing all large parties and over 75 per cent of the votes. Only one of the parties in the analysis was not part of the government in 2007 (Green Party of Switzerland), which renders government performance evaluations practically meaningless.[8] The low-clarity situation in the Czech Republic had different roots. In 2010, when the Czechs elected a new parliament, the government (led by Jan Fischer) consisted of technocrats, elected by a large party coalition. And finally, at the time of the election in Austria, the government was led by a grand coalition representing over 70 per cent of the vote shares. The two largest parties, the Social Democratic Party of Austria (SPÖ) and the Austrian People's Party (ÖVP), each had seven ministers. In these settings, attributing competence based on performance is no easy task. The low clarity of responsibility in Switzerland, the Czech Republic, and Austria might have complicated the task of deriving party competence based on government performance.

To test the robustness of this finding, I further control for the incumbency status of a party (see online appendix).[9] The effect of performance remains stable in this model. The analysis further shows that incumbency is not directly linked with competence. In twelve countries, members of the government are less likely to be rated competent. In ten countries, I find an opposite effect. Hence, simply being in government does not give parties a competitive edge with regard to issue competence. Presumably, the direction of the effect is highly situation specific.

5.4 PARTISANSHIP

The third hypothesis postulates that voters are more likely to assign competence to parties they feel close to. This is in line with the Michigan School, where party identification acts as a "perceptual screen" (Campbell et al. 1960: 133) and driver of issue evaluations. This link between partisanship and competence has been established numerous times in different settings and with varying measurements (Bélanger and Meguid 2008; Kuechler 1991; Lefevere et al. 2017; RePass 1971; Stubager and Slothuus 2013; Therriault 2015; van der Brug 2004; Wagner and Zeglovits 2014). Partisanship is measured with a binary variable indicating if the voter feels close to the party or not. Even though this is a standard variable for party adherence, most recent issue ownership studies employed different, rather unusual, measures such as a scale ranging from left-wing party identification to right-wing party identification (Stubager and Slothuus 2013) or a question asking how much a respondent agrees with the ideas of a party (Walgrave, Lefevere, and Tresch 2014).

Following H3, I expect positive γ_3 parameters. The cell entries in table 5.1 demonstrate that this is the case in all countries. This universally supports the idea that voters are likely to attribute competence to parties they feel close to. As evidenced by the HPD intervals, these results are credible on the 95 per cent level (i.e. $0 \notin$ HPD).

Visualizations of the predicted probabilities help to assess the strength of the relationship between partisanship and competence. The panels in figure 5.3 show the probability to rate a party competent (y axes) for non-partisans (left markers) and partisans (right markers). The panels are ordered based on the magnitude of the difference in predicted probabilities. In Estonia, Iceland, the Czech Republic, Austria, Finland, Slovakia, and Italy, I find vast effects of partisanship on competence (FDs >0.5). In New Zealand and Spain these effects are much smaller (FDs > 0.2). The remaining countries are quite evenly distributed between these two groups. In five countries, the FDs are between 0.4 and 0.5. In four countries, the changes in probability range between 0.3 and 0.4, and in six countries, FDs are between 0.2 and 0.3.

On the one hand, figure 5.3 confirms that the relationship between partisanship and competence is strong. On the other hand, it also shows that these increases in predicted probability often take place on a critical level. In seventeen of the twenty-four cases, the probability to rate a party competence

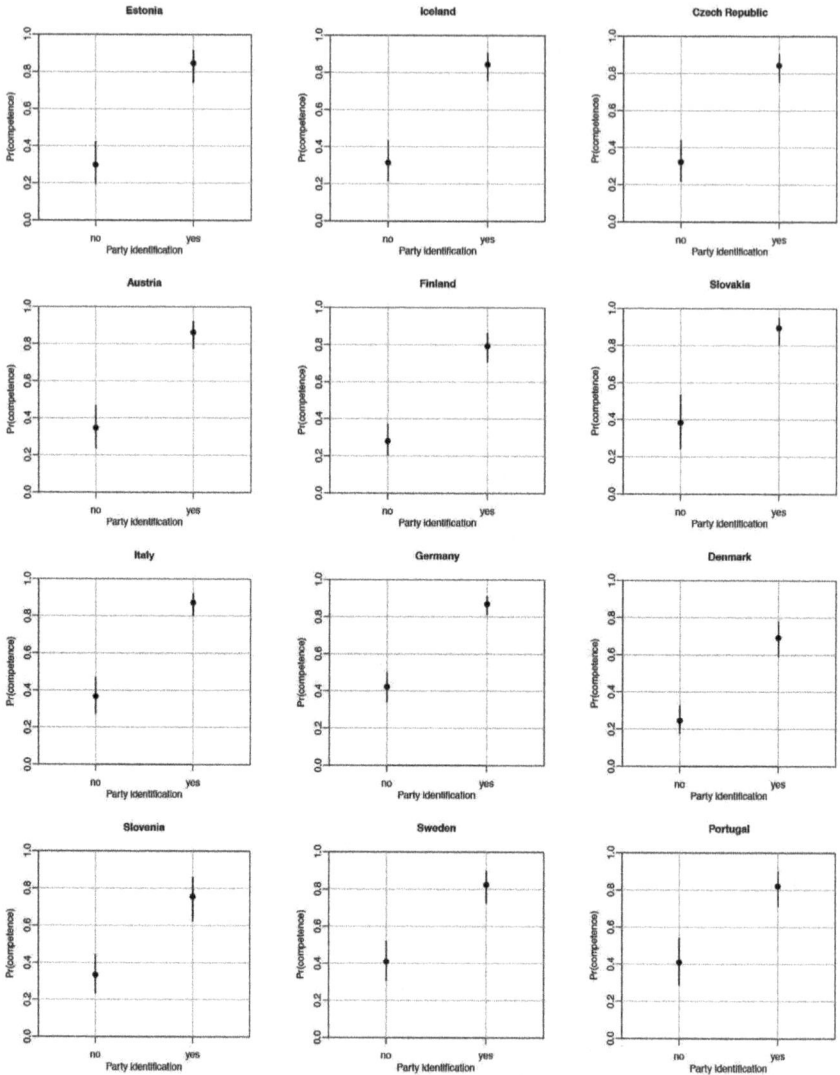

Figure 5.3. Predicted Party Competence and Partisanship.

Note: Effects estimated for the observed outcome. Whiskers = 95 per cent HPD.

Sources: CSES, ParlGov, CMP, own illustrations.

passes the threshold of 0.5 if a change from 'no partisanship' to 'partisanship' is simulated. It goes without saying that these results lend strong support for H3. In accordance with previous research, I find that partisanship is an important determinant of party competence evaluations. On average, partisanship boosts the likelihood of a positive competence rating by 0.38. This value by far exceeds the average effect of performance (0.17) or issue attention (0.07).

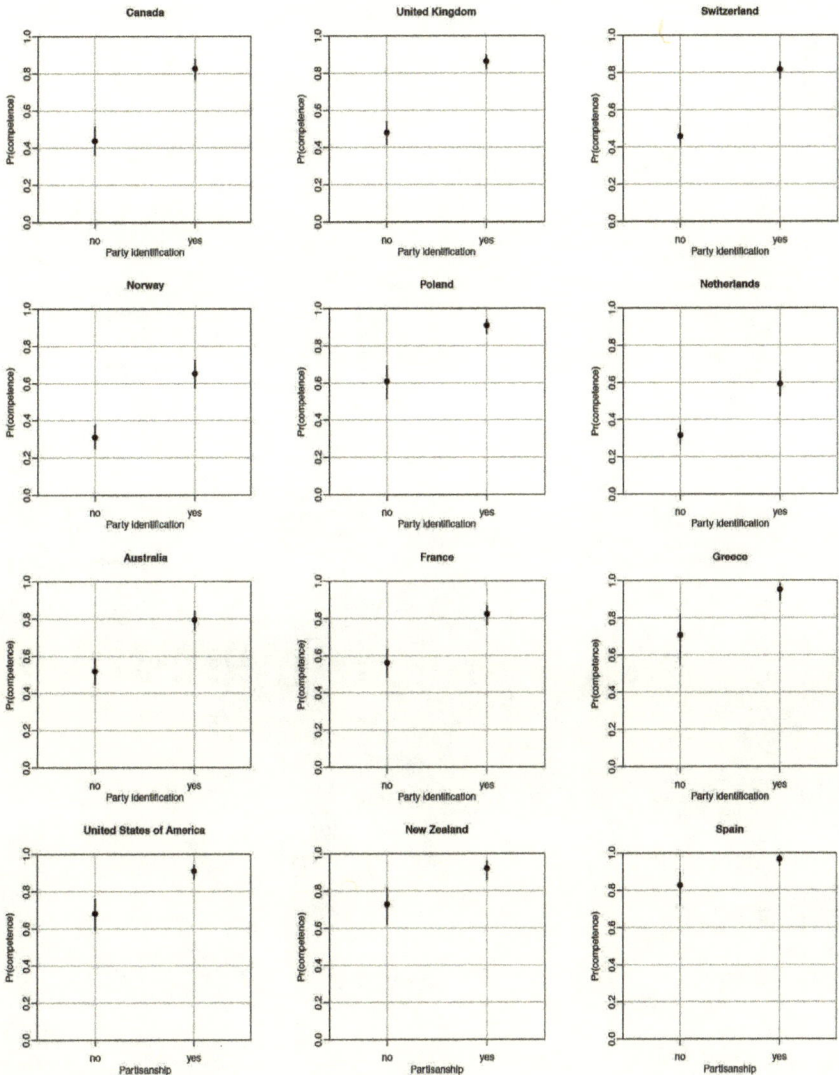

Figure 5.3. (Continued)

5.5 POSITION

In classical studies, position and competence are treated as fully distinct concepts. That is, voters are indifferent about the way a problem is solved as long as it is solved somehow (Petrocik 1996). More recent research contests this claim and shows that the difference between competence and position is not clear-cut (e.g. Stubager and Slothuus 2013; van der Brug 2004). In line with these findings, the fourth hypothesis posits that voters are less likely

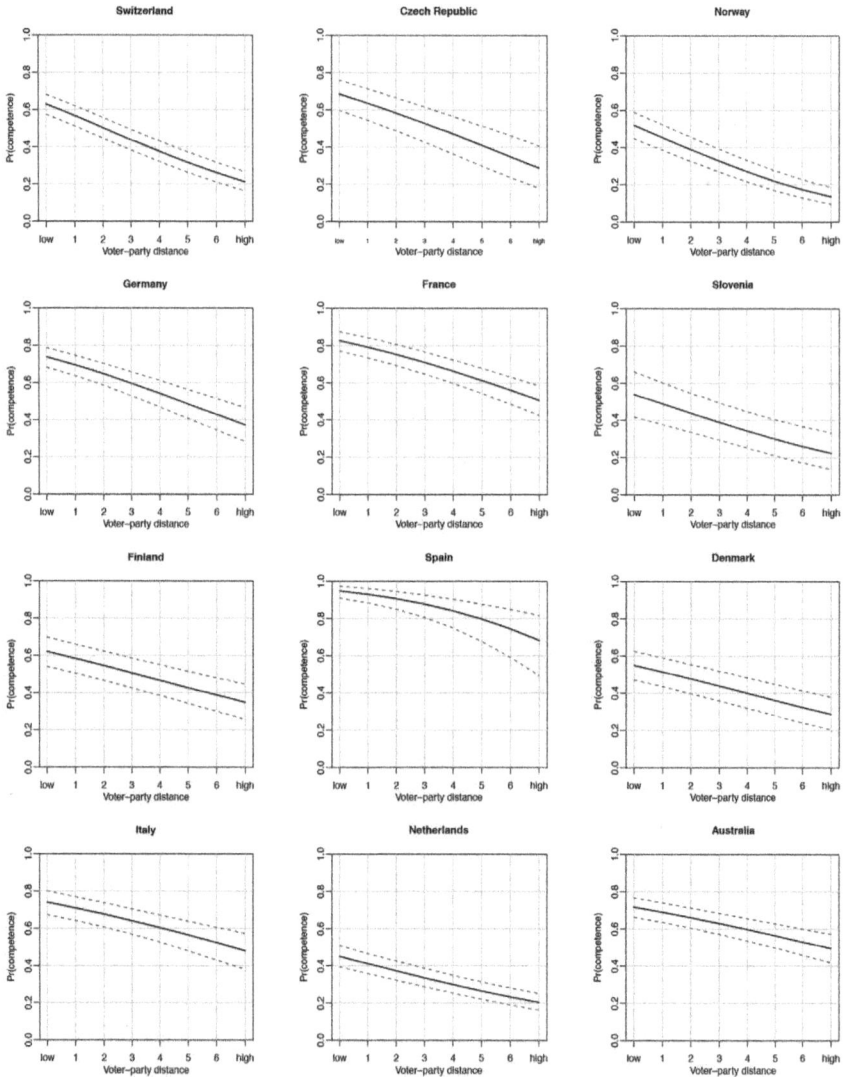

Figure 5.4. Predicted Party Competence and Voter-Party Distance.

Note: Effects estimated for the observed outcome. Dotted lines = 95 per cent HPD.

Sources: CSES, ParlGov, CMP, own illustrations.

to consider ideologically distant parties competent to handle their MIP than close parties. The key input variable is the voter-party distance on the left-right scale. High values indicate large distance between the voter and the party. H4 is supported, if γ_4 is negative. A quick glance at table 5.1 shows that this is the case and that all effects are credible.

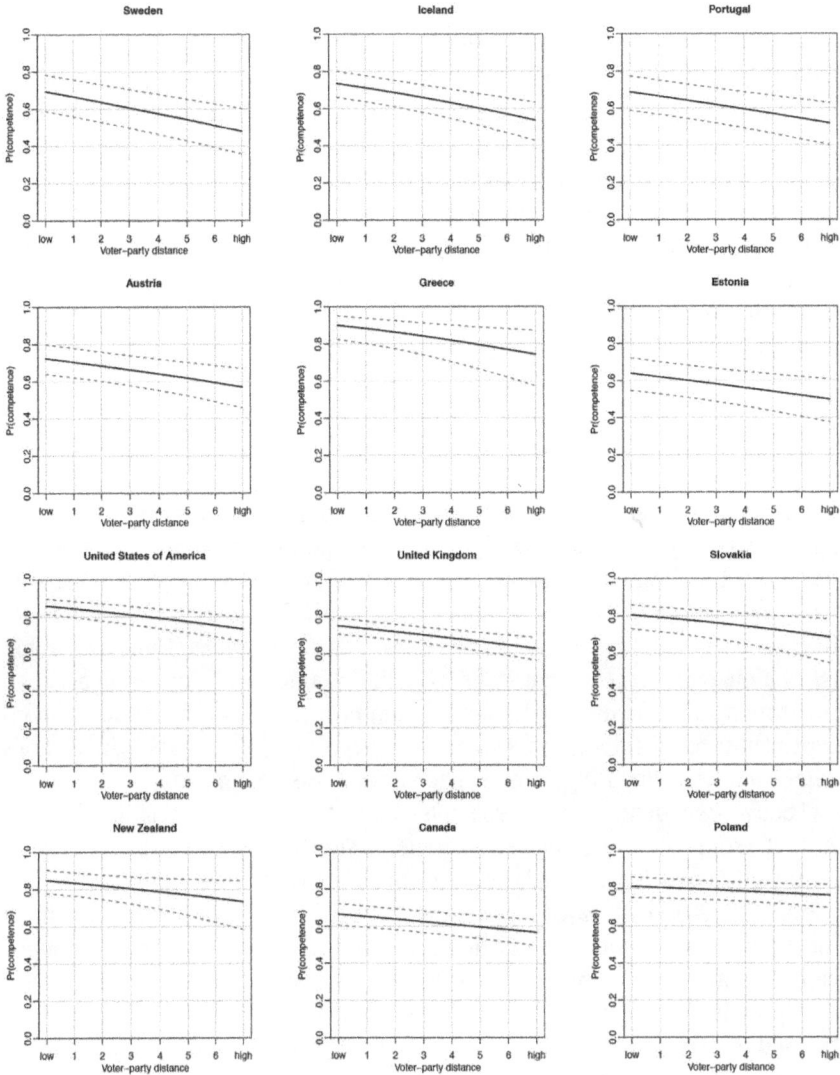

Figure 5.4. (Continued)

Figure 5.4 depicts the magnitude of these effects. It plots the probability to consider a party best at handling the MIP (*y* axes) across different levels of voter-party proximity (*x* axes). In Switzerland, position and competence are closely linked. A voter's chances to evaluate the competence of a party with the same position positively are fairly high (0.6). As the voter-party distance increases, these chances diminish. A distance of 7 points[10] lets the chances of competence assignment gravitate towards 0 (0.2). In more than half of the countries (thirteen), the FD associated with changing the distance from small (0) to large (7) is higher than 0.2. In nine cases, effects are smaller with FDs between 0.1 and 0.2. Finally, in Canada and Poland, the relationship between position and competence does not seem to be very strong (FDs <0.1). In Poland, the change in predicted probability to rate a party competent is not fully credible if the voter-party distance changes from close to far.

In sum, the results support H4. The claim that position is linked to competence is confirmed across all countries. Given these findings, a traditional conceptualization of issue ownership, where voters do not care about positions of parties when evaluating competence is hardly tenable anymore.

5.6 CONCLUSION

Thus far, the research has been largely indifferent towards the drivers of individual party competence ratings. At some point, most studies refer to the "history of attention" (Petrocik 1996: 826) as primary source of ownership. However, the reluctance to test this claim and, if necessary, propose alternative sources, led to numerous interpretations about what issue ownership is. The chapter suggests that issue ownership is not just issue emphasis and performance, nor is it just partisanship and position. It is a multifaceted concept capturing different dimensions. The degree to which these dimensions determine issue-handling competence varies across countries.

Today, two distinct measurements dominate issue ownership research. A first group of studies measures issue ownership with newspaper articles (e.g. Budge and Farlie 1983) or party manifestos (e.g. Green-Pedersen and Mortensen 2015). If party manifestos are used, ownership is equivalent to the amount of attention a party dedicates to a specific topic. The key implication of this measurement is that "issue ownership (...) is subject to party manipulation" (Meguid 2005: 349). It is a tool in the party's toolkit that can be used to gain votes. In this view, issue ownership is a product of party communication generated in a top-down process. However, none of these studies has convincingly demonstrated that issue emphasis translates well into voter perception of competence.

A second group of scholars measures issue ownership with survey questions about the competence of parties on a given topic. Survey questions do not exclude the possibility of top-down processes. Besides issue emphasis, incumbent parties could influence ownership through performance (Petrocik 1996). Accordingly, government parties are regarded competent, when they perform well on an issue. If they do not perform well, they lose ownership to opposition parties. Recent studies took a critical stand regarding the top-down perspective of issue ownership. They see competence perceptions as an expression of partisanship and ideological proximity. This would drastically lower the strategic value of issue ownership in party competition. Partisanship is a long-term affinity to a political party. Hence, it is a rather ineffective tool for short-term political campaigning. Distinct problems arise if proximity is the main driver competence. Issue ownership would no longer be a tool to generate votes outside of the ideological spectrum of the party.

In this chapter, I have examined how competence perceptions are shaped by issue emphasis (H1), government performance (H2), partisanship (H3), and ideological voter-party distance (H4). The empirical results show some evidence for a top-down perspective (H1 and H2) and much evidence for a bottom-up perspective (H3 and H4). Table 5.2 gives an overview of the results. The findings for the countries in the second column are consistent with the hypotheses. In these countries, the marginal posterior mean and the 95 per cent HPD intervals have the expected sign. The third column contains the case where the direction of the effects runs against my expectations (H1: Spain) or where the effects (positive or negative) are associated with a fair amount of uncertainty (e.g. H1: Estonia, Greece, and Italy).

The most important source of competence evaluations is *partisanship*. This effect is universal and varies hardly in strength across countries. The psychological underpinning for this can be found in research on partisan-motivated reasoning (Druckman, Peterson, and Slothuus 2013; Taber and Lodge 2006). Due to prior attitude effects, confirmation and disconfirmation bias, voters

Table 5.2. Sources of Competence: Overview Findings

Hypothesis	Confirmed	Rejected
Issue emphasis (H1)	Australia; Austria; Canada; Czech Republic; Denmark; Finland; France, Germany; Iceland; Netherlands; New Zealand; Norway; Poland; Sweden; and Switzerland	Estonia*; Greece*; Italy*; Portugal*; Slovakia*; Slovenia*; Spain; Great Britain*; and United States*
Performance (H2)	Australia; Canada; Denmark; Estonia; Finland; France; Germany; Greece; Iceland; Netherlands; New Zealand; Norway; Poland; Portugal; Slovakia; Slovenia; Spain; Sweden; and United States	Austria*; Czech Republic*; and Switzerland*
Partisanship (H3)	All countries	
Voter-party distance (H4)	All countries	

Note: Results are based on the full model (table 5.1). "Confirmed" only contains results with high credibility (0 ∉ HPD). "Rejected" contains all cases where 0 ∉ HPD (denoted with *).

use partisanship as anchor point from which they evaluate the political world. This makes it very unlikely for partisans not to pick their own party as the most competent. Further, *ideological proximity* increases the chances of a positive party competence rating in all countries. However, the effect is not as sizeable as one might suspect. In half of the countries even strong increases of voter-party distance (7 points on a 11-point scale) yield only medium changes in perceived party competence (FD <0.2).

The results for H1 and H2 are less clear-cut. Incumbent parties have some control over their ownership via *performance*. In the large majority of countries, performance shapes competence perceptions in a nontrivial way. Government parties gain competence when they are performing well and are punished for bad performances. Opposition parties suffer from good government evaluations and benefit from poor government performance. This is an important finding as it shows that competence is linked to good policy outputs and not just the product of policy expectations, partisan attachment, or promises in the party manifesto. In Switzerland, the Czech Republic, and Austria, voters do not punish or reward governing or opposition parties based on performance. Interestingly, these are low-clarity-of-responsibility cases. To substantiate how the clarity of responsibly shapes the relationship between performance and competence, further research is needed. The hypothesis on *issue emphasis* is the most ambiguous in terms of credibility and strength of the effects. In sixteen out of twenty-four countries, voters are more likely to rate a party as competent when it stresses their MIP more than all other parties. In eight countries, on the other hand, the effects are non-credible. In Spain, I even find a credible negative effect of issue attention indicating that the more attention a party devotes to an issue, the less it is regarded competent to solve it. However, even in the many cases where the hypothesis is supported, the effects are often not very strong. In eight of the sixteen cases, spending 15 percentage points more attention on an issue increases the probability to be evaluated competent by less than 0.1. This cross-country variation makes issue ownership an interesting tool in Austria, but less so in Iceland. In Austria, a 1-point increase in attention raises the probability to be regarded competent by more than 0.02. In Iceland, on the other hand, parties have to increase their issue attention by almost 15 percentage points to boost their chances of a positive competence rating by 0.002. Evidently, this puts into question the idea of issue attention as a global driver of issue ownership. This runs counter to earlier findings in the field (see e.g. Dahlberg and Martinsson 2015; Tresch, Sciarini, and Varone 2013; Walgrave, Lefevere, and Nuytemans 2009) but it supports a recent study by Stubager and Seeberg (2016). Different reasons could account for this result. First, while previous studies have focused on media data (Tresch, Sciarini, and Varone 2013; Walgrave, Lefevere, and Nuytemans 2009) or a small number of issues

(Dahlberg and Martinsson 2015), the results in this chapter are based on party manifestos and take into account a wide range of political issues. Second, it is possible that party issue attention is not well received by the voters. The motivated reasoning framework demonstrates that voters are more likely to integrate new information (i.e. a party's issue attention) if it concerns their preferred party (Lodge and Taber 2013; Taber and Lodge 2006). That is, many voters might not notice even drastic changes in issue attention if they are not attached to the party. Third, the link between what parties wish to transmit to the voters what is actually transmitted to the voters might not be as straightforward as presumed. For instance, if the translation of the manifesto into news reports is flawed, parties can put a lot of emphasis on an issue without getting credit for it.

In conclusion, these results support a critical assessment of research that (1) measures issue ownership with party manifestos or (2) treats individual issue competence perceptions as a fully independent concept unaffected by partisanship or position. Issue ownership is a multifaceted concept. In this sense, I side with Therriault (2015: 937) who notes, "Traditional issue ownership survey question should *not* be interpreted as a measurement of any one specific consideration, but instead is a reflection of various factors weighted by respondents." The present study design is different than earlier analyses by Therriault and Stubager and Slothuus. Nevertheless, I arrive at a similar conclusion. "Issue ownership is comprised of multiple distinct dimensions of public opinion, and cannot be reduced to a single concept independent of other political concerns" (Therriault 2015: 937). Or, in the words of Stubager and Slothuus (2013: 584): "Issue ownership is more than merely an expression of partisanship and attitudes."

And yet, the current debate on issue ownership centres around the idea of finding measurements that are determined by one source only. In one of the first articles on the impact of issue ownership on the vote, van der Brug (2004) notes that survey questions on competence mix general evaluations of parties, issue positions of respondents, and the priority a respondent gives to an issue. According to Walgrave et al. (2016: 783–784), unidimensionality is what we should strive for in competence ownership: "The best measure of issue ownership is one that gauges only that." Given the findings presented in this chapter and other previous analyses, I do not think that untainted evaluations of party competence are realistic, regardless of the survey question. This also relates to early analyses of issue voting, where issue evaluations were considered to be the product of multiple sources (Campbell et al. 1960; Jackson 1975; Petrocik 1996).

Chapter 6

Issue Ownership Voting

Well, I actually think this election is going to be about competence. I'm a very competent person, ok?
Donald Trump, Interview in *The Economist*, 3 September 2015

In this chapter, I look at the role of individual party competence perceptions in the decision-making process. The theoretical framework describes issue ownership voting as voting based on the evaluation of a party's competence to handle an important issue (H5). As of today, issue ownership voting studies are mostly national (Lefevere et al. 2017: 3). The rare analyses with a comparative approach do not study the vote choice in national elections. I seek to fill this gap by investigating competence-based voting in twenty-four countries, in many of which issue ownership voting has never been studied in the context of a national legislative election.

After examining the basic issue ownership voting hypothesis, I turn to the question how partisanship and ideological distance between voter and party moderates this type of voting. I argue that both partisanship and voter-party distance dampen competence-based voting (H6 and H7). This claim rests on two arguments. First, both factors are strong predictors of the vote choice on their own right. Voters who share the same ideology with a party or partisans are likely to support their party at the election polls, regardless of their competence rating.

However, rating a party competent despite having a distinct ideological position should have a strong impact on the vote. Similarly, nonpartisans cannot rely on partisanship when making a decision. These citizens have to rely on other cues, which is why the effect of competence should be stronger.

The results show that party competence ratings are an important driver of the vote choice in all countries. Moreover, I find that partisanship and ideological proximity decrease the effect of competence on the voting decision in the majority of countries.

6.1 METHOD

In the empirical analysis, I use data from the CSES and the CMP. To measure a party's incumbency status, I rely on the ParlGov.

The outcome in the analysis is 'party choice', a nominal variable with the categories; $j = 1, \ldots, J$. The number of parties in a country varies between two and seven and amounts to 117 in total (table 4.3). On average, these parties represent 90 per cent of the vote shares (table 4.4). The main input variable is an individual's 'party competence evaluation', which has the same alternatives (parties) as the vote choice. This indicator, as well as the controls 'partisanship', 'voter-party distance', 'government performance', and 'party issue attention' varies across voter $i = 1, \ldots, n$ and choice alternative (x_{ij}). Variables of this type are commonly analysed in conditional logit regression models. They are represented by a matrix, where the number of columns equals the number of parties in a country. The respondent's gender, age, education, political sophistication, and the MIP are constant across the categories of the outcome variable but vary across individuals (x_i). Scholars usually estimate effects of such variables on a categorical outcome in MNLM. As in the previous chapter, I rely on hybrid regression models. Unlike pure CLM and MNLM, these models estimate effects of party-specific and voter-specific variables. This is an important advantage as settling for one type of variable would result in an underspecified model of the vote choice. The hybrid model is based on the random utility theory, where functions are estimated to describe a voter's gain from choosing one party over the other. According to the axiom of utility maximization, the voter selects j if $U_{ij} > U_{ik}, \forall k \neq j$. The model contains a stochastic component (ϵ_{ij}) and a systematic component (V_{ij}).[1]

The first set of models controls for the respondent's 'gender', 'age', 'education', and 'political sophistication'. As discussed in the theoretical framework, the valence part of an issue might vary (section 3.2.1). Claiming that issue ownership voting affects all issues equally is clearly a simplification of De Sio and Weber's (2014) nuanced claim. In an attempt to tackle this problem, all models control for the MIP.[2] The systematic part of the baseline models is specified as follows (equation 6.1):

$$
\begin{aligned}
V_{ij} = \ &\beta_{0j} + \beta_{1j} \cdot \text{age}_i + \beta_{2j} \cdot \text{sex}_i + \beta_{3j} \cdot \text{education}_i + \beta_{4j} \cdot \text{sophistication}_i \\
&+ \beta_{5j} \cdot \text{social}_i + \beta_{6j} \cdot \text{external}_i + \beta_{7j} \cdot \text{services}_i + \beta_{8j} \cdot \text{immigration}_i \\
&+ \beta_{9j} \cdot \text{quality}_i + \beta_{10j} \cdot \text{other}_i + \beta_{11j} \cdot \text{security}_i \\
&+ \gamma_1 \cdot \text{competence}_{ij}
\end{aligned}
\qquad (6.1)
$$

where competence$_{ij}$ indicates whether voter i rates party j as best capable of handling the MIP or not. These models set the baseline for the effect of competence ratings on the vote decision. However, as demonstrated in the previous chapter, partisanship, voter-party distance, performance and, to some degree, party issue attention shape competence evaluations. A second set of full models controls forhese indicators and takes the following form (equation 6.2):

$$
\begin{aligned}
V_{ijc} = {} & \beta_{0j} + \beta_{1j} \cdot \text{age}_i + \beta_{2j} \cdot \text{sex}_i + \beta_{3j} \cdot \text{education}_i + \beta_{4j} \cdot \text{sophistication}_i \\
& + \beta_{5j} \cdot \text{social}_i + \beta_{6jc} \cdot \text{external}_i + \beta_{7jc} \cdot \text{services}_i + \beta_{8j} \cdot \text{immigration}_i \\
& + \beta_{9j} \cdot \text{quality}_i + \beta_{10j} \cdot \text{other}_i + \beta_{11j} \cdot \text{security}_i \\
& + \gamma_1 \cdot \text{competence}_{ij} + \gamma_2 \cdot \text{partisan}_{ij} + \gamma_3 \cdot \text{distance}_{ij} + \gamma_4 \cdot \text{performance}_{ij} \\
& + \gamma_5 \cdot \text{attention}_{ij}
\end{aligned} \tag{6.2}
$$

where partisan$_{ij}$ measures an individual's party identification, distance$_{ij}$ measures the spatial distance between voter and the parties, performance$_{ij}$ is the performance of the government party, and attention$_{ij}$ is the share of party j's manifesto dedicated to the voter's MIP. The aim of these models is to demonstrate that the positive relationship between competence and the vote choice persists, even if I control for alternative voting theories. In a strict sense, they show if competence ratings further our understanding of the vote choice beyond what we already know from other approaches.

I then turn to the question how voter-party distance and partisanship moderate issue ownership voting. The corresponding model is specified in equation 6.3:

$$
\begin{aligned}
V_{ijc} = {} & \beta_{0j} + \beta_{1j} \cdot \text{age}_i + \beta_{2j} \cdot \text{sex}_i + \beta_{3j} \cdot \text{education}_i + \beta_{4j} \cdot \text{sophistication}_i \\
& + \beta_{5j} \cdot \text{social}_i + \beta_{6jc} \cdot \text{external}_i + \beta_{7j} \cdot \text{services}_i + \beta_{8j} \cdot \text{immigration}_i \\
& + \beta_{9j} \cdot \text{quality}_i + \beta_{10j} \cdot \text{other}_i + \beta_{11j} \cdot \text{security}_i \\
& + \gamma_1 \cdot \text{competence}_{ij} + \gamma_2 \cdot \text{partisan}_{ij} + \gamma_3 \cdot \text{competence\_partisan}_{ij} \\
& + \gamma_4 \cdot \text{distance}_{ij} + \gamma_5 \cdot \text{performance}_{ij} + \gamma_6 \cdot \text{attention}_{ij}
\end{aligned} \tag{6.3}
$$

where competence_partisan$_{ij}$ is an interaction term between partisanship and competence evaluation. Negative γ_3 parameters indicate that partisanship decreases competence-based voting. A final set of models interacts competence evaluations with voter-party distance (i.e. competence_partisan$_{ij}$ turns into competence_distance$_{ij}$). In this case, positive γ_3 parameters show that increasing voter-party distance reinforces issue ownership voting.

All models are implemented in a Bayesian framework. The estimations are done with the package rjags for R (Plummer 2016). I specify vague $N(0,10^2)$

priors for γ and β. Due to autocorrelation, I run long chains of 150,000 its. with a burn-in of 50,000 its.

The regression tables do not list parameters that are constant across parties. Such parameters are hard to interpret and impractical to present. Summarizing the full model would result in twenty-four tables with an average of five columns (one for each party) and twelve parameters per column. Like in the previous chapter, I discuss the results based on predicted probabilities and FDs. Suppose I want to approximate the probability to support a given party in a country. In this case, I first run the MCMC and store the 150,000 draws for γ and β. I then multiply these draws with the observed values of all variables for each voter in the sample and calculate the predicted probability. I only estimate the predicted probability to support the observed party choice; that is, when voter i casts his or her ballot for party j, the value shows the predicted probability to support this party.[3] This yields 150,000 predicted probabilities per survey participant, which I aggregate on the voter level and then average across all voters. The same is done with the 97.5th and 2.5th percentiles of the predicted probabilities. These two values span the 95 per cent HPD region. The differences in predicted probabilities are estimated by comparing the predicted probabilities of the same voter when only the variable of interest is changed. In the present case, this means estimating 150,000 predicted probabilities for each voter and scenario (e.g. 'the respondent rates the party he or she voted for best able to deal with the MIP' and 'the respondent rates another party competent'). The FD is calculated by averaging the differences between these two scenarios on the voter level and then across all voters.

6.2 ISSUE OWNERSHIP VOTING

All baseline models (equation 6.1) are presented in table 6.1. The values summarize the marginal posterior densities of party competence evaluations (γ_1) and their 95 per cent HPD. The sign of an effect is credible if the HPD does not contain the value zero ($0 \notin$ HPD). The countries are alphabetically ordered. Party competence evaluation takes the value 1 if the voter rates the party competent to handle the top issue and takes the value 0 otherwise. Hence, the issue ownership voting hypothesis (H5) is supported if the regression parameters are positive, that is, if a favourable competence evaluation increases the probability to vote for a party. Table 6.1 shows that this is the case in every country. The HPDs, moreover, suggest that these effects are highly credible. This means that a voter's chance to support a party increases if he or she rates the party competent to handle the most important political problem.

Table 6.1. Issue Ownership Voting: Baseline Models

Country	Competence, γ	γ HPD	Controls
Australia	2.09	[1.95, 2.24]	✓
Austria	2.44	[2.22, 2.68]	✓
Canada	1.91	[1.77, 2.05]	✓
Czech Republic	2.51	[2.31, 2.71]	✓
Denmark	2.56	[2.38, 2.74]	✓
Estonia	2.31	[2.07, 2.56]	✓
Finland	2.71	[2.54, 2.89]	✓
France	1.78	[1.63, 1.94]	✓
Germany	2.36	[2.21, 2.50]	✓
Greece	3.14	[2.64, 3.72]	✓
Iceland	2.44	[2.25, 2.65]	✓
Italy	2.39	[2.18, 2.61]	✓
Netherlands	2.26	[2.13, 2.39]	✓
New Zealand	2.47	[2.11, 2.88]	✓
Norway	2.05	[1.90, 2.20]	✓
Poland	2.25	[2.07, 2.45]	✓
Portugal	2.17	[1.93, 2.43]	✓
Slovakia	3.11	[2.82, 3.42]	✓
Slovenia	1.81	[1.48, 2.15]	✓
Spain	2.44	[2.17, 2.73]	✓
Sweden	2.98	[2.71, 3.25]	✓
Switzerland	1.83	[1.69, 1.96]	✓
United Kingdom	1.83	[1.70, 1.92]	✓
United States	1.57	[1.42, 1.72]	✓

Note: Marginal posterior densities of γ (equation 6.1). Numbers in brackets are 95 per cent HPD. MCMC with 150,000 it. after 50,000 it. burn-in.

Sources: CSES, ParlGov and own calculations.

Let us now turn to the full models (equation 6.2). Table 6.2 reports the parameters for party competence evaluation (γ_1), emphasis of the MIP (γ_2), performance (γ_3), partisanship (γ_4), and voter-party distance (γ_5). First, all γ_1 parameters keep their positive sign. This lends support for the hypothesis that rating a party best at handling the MIP increases the probability to support the party at the ballot box. Furthermore, none of the HPD regions span negative values, which show that the sign of the parameters is credible. Compared to the baseline models, the parameters decrease in size. That is, the effect of competence evaluations decreases once partisanship, voter-party distance, issue attention, and party performance are controlled for. This is not surprising, given that these covariates are related to competence evaluations (chapter 5).

In eight countries (Denmark, France, Germany, Greece, Norway, Poland, Spain, and Switzerland), *issue emphasis* has a positive and credible effect on

Table 6.2. Issue Ownership Voting: Full Models

Country	Comp., y_1	Emph., y_2	Perf., y_3	PI, y_4	Dist., y_5	Cont.
Australia	1.25	-0.02	0.44	2.27	-0.19	✓
	[1.05, 1.44]	[-0.07, 0.02]	[0.28, 0.60]	[2.08, 2.48]	[-0.26, -0.11]	
Austria	1.23	-0.05	0.11	2.90	-0.02	✓
	[0.94, 1.54]	[-0.11, 0.01]	[-0.10, 0.30]	[2.55, 3.27]	[-0.12, 0.08]	
Canada	0.95	-0.02	-0.21	1.95	-0.16	✓
	[0.78, 1.13]	[-0.04, 0.01]	[-0.33, -0.08]	[1.76, 2.14]	[-0.21, -0.11]	
Czech Republic	1.33	-0.02	0.09	2.27	-0.28	✓
	[1.08, 1.58]	[-0.14, 0.09]	[-0.16, 0.35]	[1.97, 2.59]	[-0.37, -0.20]	
Denmark	1.56	0.02	-0.08	2.99	-0.32	✓
	[1.30, 1.82]	[0.00, 0.04]	[-0.29, 0.12]	[2.73, 3.26]	[-0.41, -0.23]	
Estonia	1.40	0.02	0.22	2.24	-0.12	✓
	[1.09, 1.71]	[-0.08, 0.11]	[-0.01, 0.45]	[1.85, 2.65]	[-0.22, -0.02]	
Finland	1.45	0.00	0.15	2.72	-0.14	✓
	[1.22, 1.67]	[-0.02, 0.01]	[-0.01, 0.31]	[2.48, 2.96]	[-0.23, -0.06]	
France	0.58	0.06	0.06	1.41	-0.30	✓
	[0.37, 0.79]	[0.02, 0.11]	[-0.08, 0.19]	[1.21, 1.61]	[-0.37, -0.23]	
Germany	1.31	0.08	0.16	1.67	-0.23	✓
	[1.13, 1.49]	[0.04, 0.16]	[0.03, 0.28]	[1.47, 1.87]	[-0.30, -0.16]	
Greece	1.23	0.05	-0.01	3.32	-0.19	✓
	[0.58, 1.94]	[0.00, 0.10]	[-0.32, 0.27]	[2.63, 4.10]	[-0.38, 0.00]	
Iceland	1.37	0.01	0.07	1.86	-0.11	✓
	[1.12, 1.62]	[-0.02, 0.04]	[-0.09, 0.23]	[1.57, 2.15]	[-0.20, -0.02]	
Italy	1.32	-0.02		2.26	-0.12	✓
	[1.05, 1.59]	[-0.05, 0.01]		[1.95, 2.60]	[-0.20, -0.04]	
Netherlands	1.95	-0.01	0.43	2.35	-0.28	✓
	[1.78, 2.12]	[-0.07, 0.04]	[0.21, 0.67]	[2.18, 2.52]	[-0.33, -0.23]	
New Zealand	1.50	0.01	0.26	1.93	-0.18	✓
	[1.05, 2.00]	[-0.03, 0.05]	[0.01, 0.53]	[1.47, 2.44]	[-0.39, 0.03]	

Norway	1.29 [1.12, 1.46]	0.08 [0.04, 0.12]	0.37 [0.17, 0.58]	2.19 [1.96, 2.42]	-0.39 [-0.45, -0.33]	✓
Poland	1.12 [0.89, 1.36]	0.03 [0.00, 0.06]	0.35 [0.18, 0.52]	1.64 [1.39, 1.90]	-0.17 [-0.25, -0.09]	✓
Portugal	1.44 [1.14, 1.75]	-0.04 [-0.10, 0.09]	0.17 [-0.01, 0.36]	1.41 [1.08, 1.76]	-0.04 [-0.13, 0.06]	✓
Slovakia	1.27 [0.89, 1.64]	0.07 [-0.02, 0.13]	0.20 [-0.06, 0.47]	2.78 [2.40, 3.18]	-0.08 [-0.21, 0.05]	✓
Slovenia	1.24 [0.88, 1.62]	-0.21 [-0.34, -0.09]	0.47 [0.21, 0.74]	2.11 [1.33, 2.96]	-0.08 [-0.21, 0.05]	✓
Spain	1.03 [0.57, 1.48]	0.47 [0.20, 1.09]	0.26 [0.00, 0.51]	1.05 [0.54, 1.58]	-0.34 [-0.48, -0.20]	✓
Sweden	1.69 [1.31, 2.08]	-0.05 [-0.14, 0.01]	0.41 [0.06, 0.80]	2.92 [2.54, 3.33]	-0.22 [-0.35, -0.09]	✓
Switzerland	1.12 [0.96, 1.28]	0.03 [0.02, 0.04]	0.04 [-0.16, 0.24]	1.93 [1.74, 2.13]	-0.21 [-0.25, -0.16]	✓
United Kingdom	0.84 [0.67, 1.01]	0.02 [-0.03, 0.07]		1.97 [1.81, 2.14]	-0.06 [-0.13, 0.00]	✓
United States	0.88 [0.70, 1.06]	0.04 [-0.01, 0.10]	0.18 [0.09, 0.28]	1.12 [0.94, 1.30]	-0.03 [-0.07, 0.02]	✓

Note: Marginal posterior densities of γ (equation 6.2). Numbers in brackets are 95 per cent HPD. MCMC with 150,000 it. after 50,000 it. burn-in. comp. = competence, emph. = party issue emphasis, perf. = government performance, dist. = voter-party distance, PI = party identification, cont. = control variables.

Sources: CSES, ParlGov, CMP, and own calculations.

Chapter 6

the vote. In these cases, the likelihood to vote for a party is positively linked to the amount of attention this party spends on the voter's MIP in the manifesto. However, this is by no means a universal finding. In two-thirds of the countries, the effects of issue attention are either not credible or even negative (Slovenia). In nine countries, *party performance* yields a positive and credible effect on the vote (γ_3). That is, evaluating the performance of an incumbent party favourably increases the probability to support this party at the polls and decreases the chances to vote for the opposition. Again, these results are not clear-cut. In ten countries, the positive effects are not credible; in Canada, Denmark, and Greece the MCMC chain picks up negative (though not credible) parameters. *Partisanship* is positive and credible in all countries (γ_4). Voters are more likely to support a party if they have a long-standing attachment to the party. With the exception of Portugal, the effects of partisanship are stronger than the effects of party competence (i.e. $\gamma_4 > \gamma_1$). Thus, from a party's perspective, partisanship is electorally more rewarding than being competent on a voter's MIP. However, given that competence ratings are more volatile than partisanship and, to a limited extent, subject to manipulation, issue ownership voting might be more interesting to a political campaigner than partisanship. Finally, all γ_5 parameters in table 6.2 have the expected negative sign. A voter's probability to support a party decreases, as the *voter-party distance* on the left-right axis increases. This finding is not credible on a 95 per cent level in Austria, Greece, New Zealand, Portugal, Slovakia, and the United States. Ideological distance is a continuous covariate. The parameters show the effect of a one-unit increase in voter-party distance. If we travel the entire scale from the minimal (0) to the maximal theoretical score (11), the proximity model may be as important as issue ownership voting or partisanship voting. However, I do not observe this maximal in any of the countries.

The above discussion has shown that issue ownership voting takes place in all countries. I now turn to the question how strong the effect of party competence on the vote is. The panels in figure 6.1 show the probability to support a party if it is not regarded best able to handle the MIP (markers on the left) and if it is regarded competent on the MIP (markers on the right). Triangle markers are derived from the baseline models and round markers from the full models. Note that the values denote the probability to vote for the party the respondent actually supported at the election. The panels are ordered according to the results of full models so that countries with the largest differences in predicted probabilities between the scenario 'party competent' and the scenario 'party not competent' appear first (the Netherlands, Germany, and Portugal); countries with the smallest differences in predicted probabilities are presented last (France, Greece, and Spain).

Let us begin with the baseline models, where voters have a low probability to vote for a party if they *do not rate it competent* to handle an important issue. In this case, the number of parties competing in an election appears to drive the probabilities. In countries with only two parties (Spain, the United States, and New Zealand), the probability to vote for a party is around 0.5. In multiparty systems, such as the Netherlands, Finland, Norway, or Denmark, these probabilities are much smaller (around 0.2). In the scenario 'party not

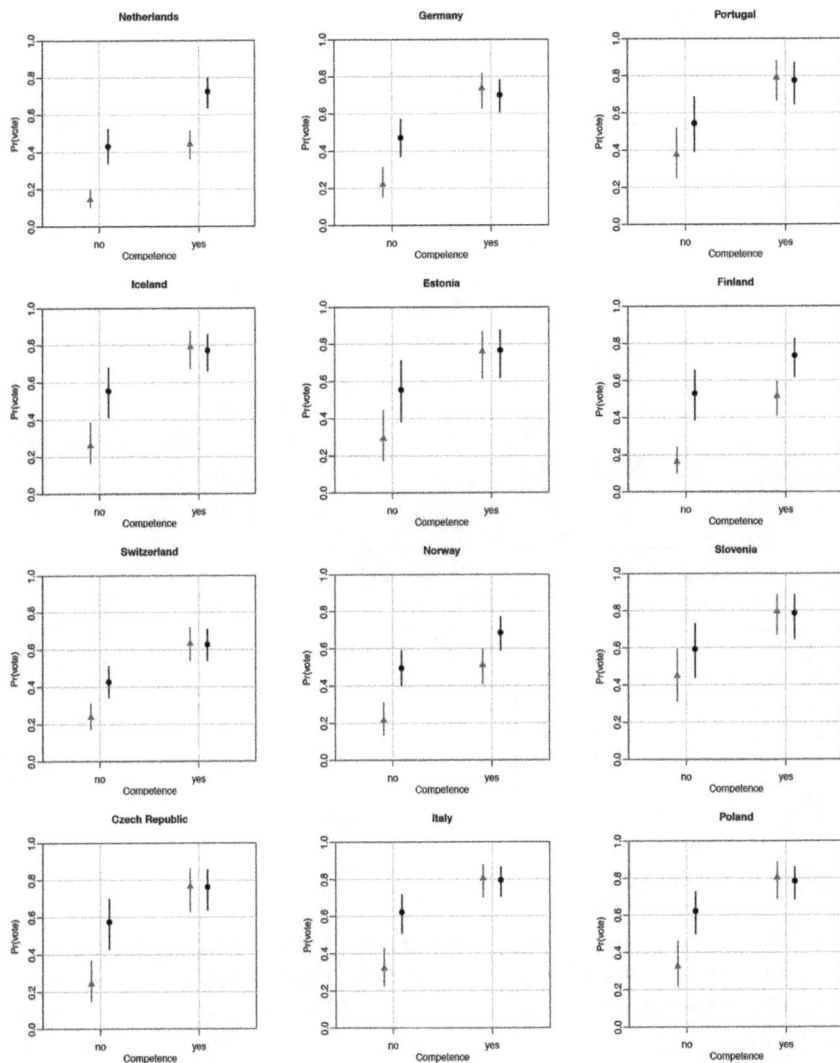

Figure 6.1. Predicted Vote Choice and Party Competence. *Sources*: CSES, ParlGov, CMP, and own illustrations.

Note: Effects estimated for the observed outcome. Whiskers = 95 per cent HPDs. Triangle markers = baseline models, round markers = full models.

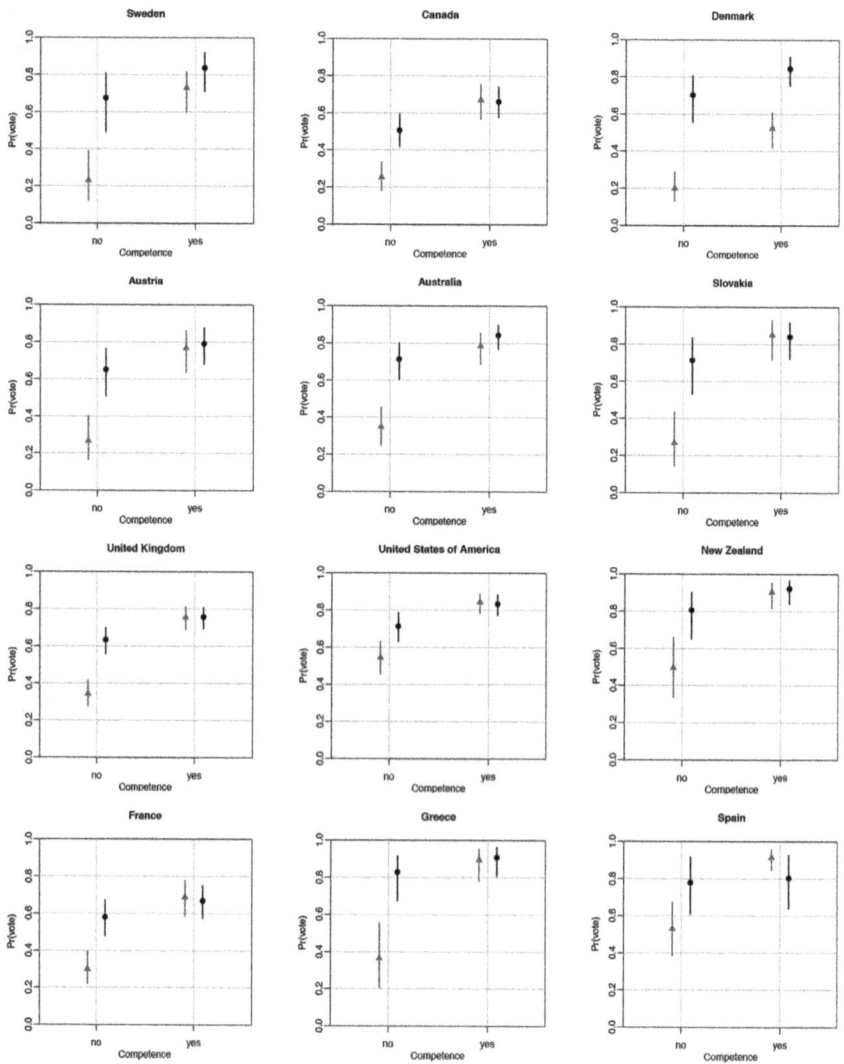

Figure 6.1. (Continued)

competent', the probability of party support increases sharply, once I introduce alternative explanations of the vote choice (full models). With the exceptions of the Netherlands, Germany, Switzerland, and Norway, the probability
to support a party is above 0.5, even when the voter does not rate the party
as competent. This links to the estimation of the predicted probabilities. In
the observed-value approach, all input variables (with the exception of party
competence) take their observed value. This gives a more realistic account of
the effects than the widely used average-case approach (Hanmer and Ozan

Kalkan 2013). Given that the control variables take their actual value, many predicted probabilities are estimated for partisans and respondents where the voter-party distance is small. Since these variables are strong predictors of the vote choice themselves, the probability to support the observed party is high, even when the competence rating is not positive. In the *competent scenario*, the probabilities often do not differ much between the two models. An exception is again multiparty systems (the Netherlands, Finland, Norway, and Denmark), where the probability of party support remains below 0.6 in the baseline model, even when the party is evaluated competent on the MIP.

Figure 6.2 visualizes the increase in predicted probability associated with changing the party evaluation from 'not competent' to 'competent'. The round markers are based on the full models; triangle markers show FDs from the baseline models.[4] The panel on the right-hand side shows the difference between the full and the baseline models. Whereas in the case of the Netherlands the FD remains largely the same in both models, the impact of competence decreases strongly in Slovakia and Greece, once alternative explanations of the vote are controlled for.

If we consider the full model on the left-hand side of figure 6.2 (round markers), it becomes clear that the level of competence-based voting varies across the countries. In the Netherlands, the probability to vote for a party increases by almost 0.3, if we move from a scenario where the party is not rated competent to a scenario where it is seen as competent on the MIP. In seven countries, this premium is higher than 0.2. In the majority of the cases (fourteen countries), the FD is between 0.1 and 0.2.

In France, Greece, and Spain, competence pays smaller electoral dividends (FDs <0.1). These values are all much larger in the baseline model (triangle markers). On average, the FD decreases by 0.27 in the full model compared to the baseline model. Hence, other voting strategies such as partisanship voting, proximity voting, or performance voting explain a considerable part of the effects in the baseline model. Despite this, the average FD in the full models remains high (0.16) and credible on the 95 per cent level. This important finding demonstrates that the introduction of party competence ratings improves standard models of vote choice in all examined countries.

These findings hold even when I use alternative measurements for partisanship and voter-party distance. Instead of a binary variable indicating whether an individual feels close to a specific party or not, the analyses provided in the online appendix use a 10-point sympathy score to measure partisanship. These models, moreover, differ from those presented earlier in the way they measure party positions. When calculating the voter-party distance, they substitute expert scores with individual perceptions of party positions. This yields a more subjective score for spatial distance between voters and parties. The results regarding issue ownership voting are robust to these alternative

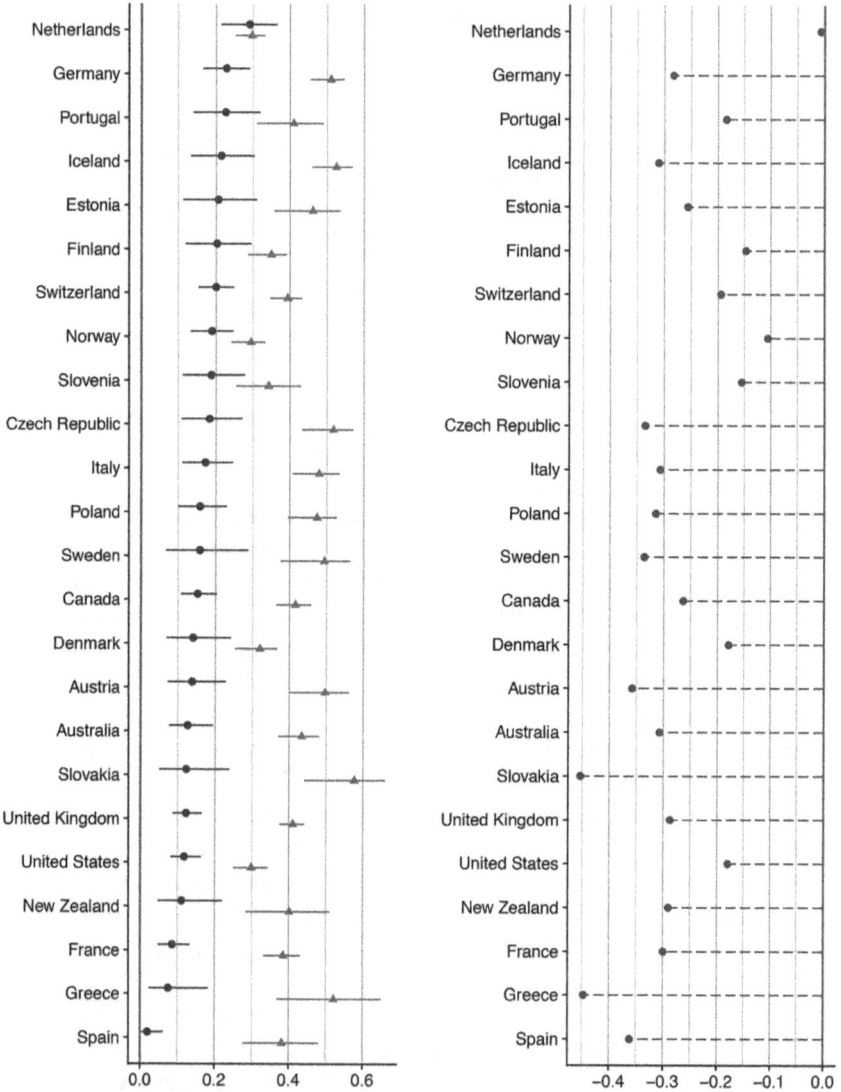

Figure 6.2. First Differences and Change between Baseline Models and Full Models. *Sources*: CSES, ParlGov, CMP, and own illustrations.

Note: Left: FDs associated with changing party competence from 'not competent' to 'competent'. Round markers = full models; triangle markers = baseline models. Whiskers = 95 per cent HPD. Right: Difference between the baseline model and the full model. Negative values indicate that the FD in the full model is smaller than in the baseline models.

specifications. The competence parameters in the regression tables and FDs remain positive and highly credible.

In a final step, I estimate the effect of competence ratings in a full model across all countries.[5] Given the clear support for the issue ownership voting

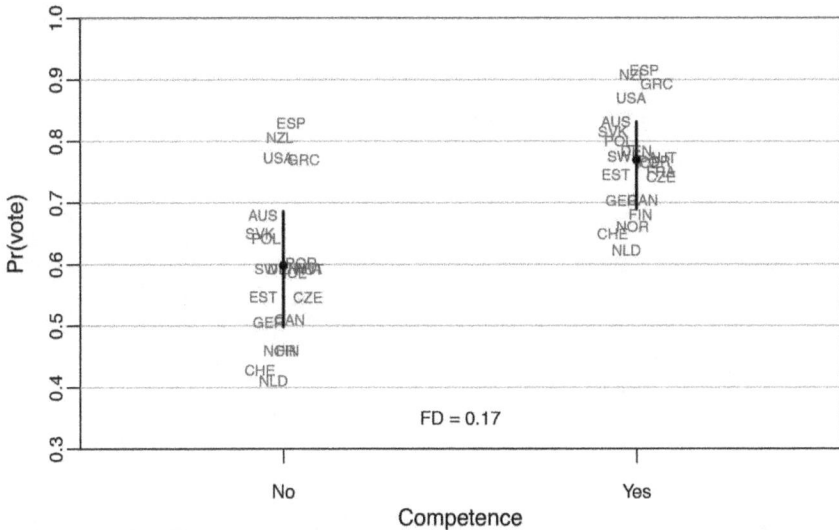

Figure 6.3. Predicted Vote Choice and Party Competence (All Countries). *Sources*: CSES, ParlGov, CMP, and own illustrations.

hypothesis in the country-specific models, it does not come as a surprise that the effect of competence in this hierarchical model is positive and credible as well. Across all elections, the increase in predicted probability associated with a positive competence rating amounts to 0.17 (figure 6.3).

6.3 THE MODERATING EFFECT OF IDEOLOGY AND PARTISANSHIP

In this section, I tackle the question how ideological proximity and partisanship moderate issue ownership voting. I expect partisanship to decrease (H6), and high ideological voter-party distance to increase (H7) competence-based voting. Given that several researchers have pointed out the limitations of interpreting additive interaction terms in logistic regression models (Brambor, Clark, and Golder 2006; Friedrich 1982; Kam and Franzese 2007), I base the discussion entirely on visualizations of the results. Tables containing the interactions and their constitutive terms are provided in the online appendix. H6 presumes that partisanship lowers the effect of competence evaluations on the vote. First, we should observe a ceiling effect. Partisans are already likely to support their party, regardless of their competence evaluation. Furthermore, compared to partisans, nonpartisans lack an important cue to form a decision (namely their attachment to a party). Hence, they have to rely on alternative decision-making strategies such as issue voting.

Figure 6.4 shows the FDs changing the competence evaluation (from 'not competent' to 'competent') for nonpartisans (round markers) and for partisans (triangle markers). The overall picture is unambiguous. First, for nonpartisans, the impact of competence on the vote is high. On average, the

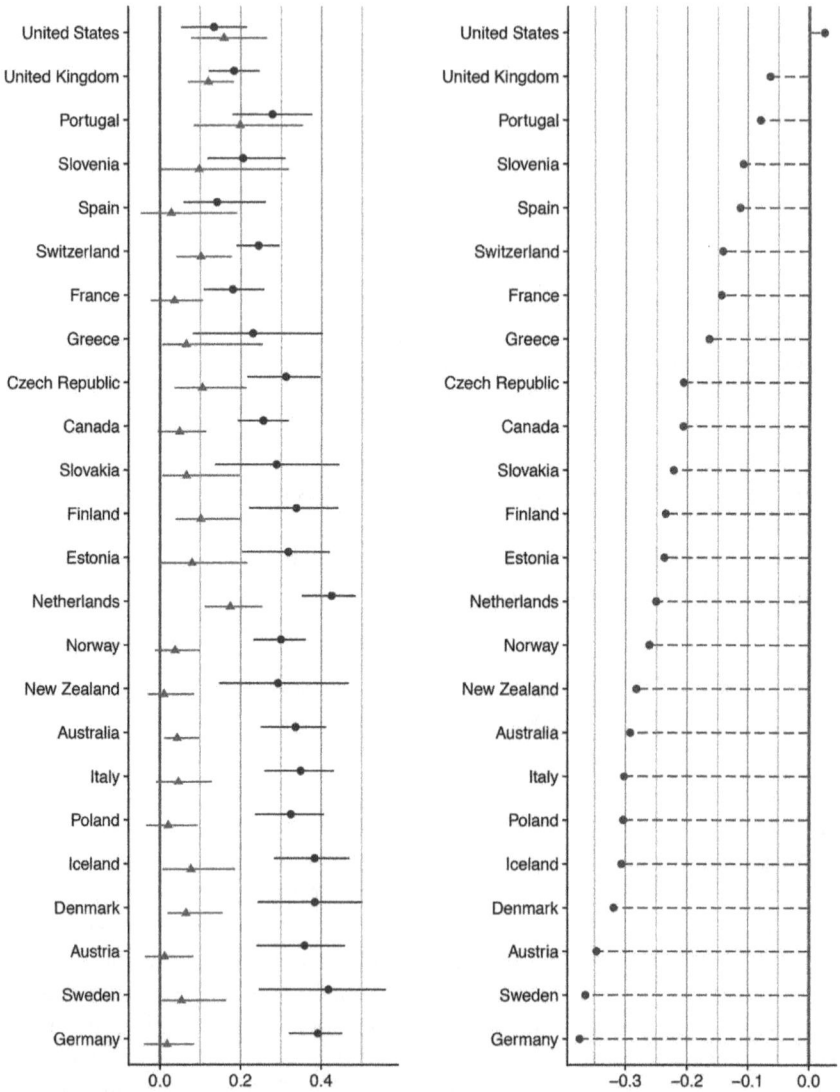

Figure 6.4. First Differences: Interaction Partisanship. *Sources*: CSES, ParlGov, CMP, and own illustrations.

Note: Left: FDs associated with changing party competence from 'not competent' to 'competent'. Round markers = nonpartisans; triangle markers = partisans. Whiskers = 95 per cent HPDs. Right: Difference between the two voter types. Negative values indicate a stronger effect of competence for nonpartisans.

probability to support a party increases by 0.29 if the party is best capable of handling the MIP. Second, for partisans, the average FD amounts to merely 0.07. Moreover, in eleven out of the twenty-four countries, I find no support of the issue ownership voting hypothesis for partisans. The panel on the right-hand side of figure 6.4 shows the differences between the effects. Markers on the left of the horizontal line indicate that partisanship decreases competence-based voting. On average, the FDs are 0.22 smaller for partisans. This lends support to the idea that nonpartisans lean heavily on competence evaluations when taking their decision. Partisans, on the other hand, do not rely on competence as much. A partisan's average probability to support his or her party is 0.82, even when he or she does not see the party best capable of handling the MIP. However, for nonpartisans, competence evaluations are of utmost importance when forming their decision. In twenty out of the twenty-four countries, the predicted probability passes the threshold of 0.5 when competence changes from 'not competent' to 'competent'.

Let us now turn to ideological proximity and its role in competence-based voting. The left panel in figure 6.5 depicts the increases in predicted probability as the competence evaluation for a party changes from not 'competent' to 'competent'. These FDs are calculated for voters whose voter-party distance on the left-right axis is large (4, round markers) and for voters whose ideological distance is small (0, triangle markers). The panel on the right shows the differences between these effects. Markers on the right of the vertical line indicate that issue ownership voting is reinforced when voter-party distance is small; markers on the left show that issue ownership voting is more common when the voter has a different ideology than the party.

A first important result is that the positive effect of issue ownership remains credible in most countries, regardless of the ideological distance. Exceptions are Spain, Greece, France, and the United States, where the effect of competence on the vote is not fully credible for voters who feel close to the party. Second, in all but four countries (Slovenia, Italy, Slovakia, and Poland), issue ownership voting is stronger when the ideological distance between voter and party is large. On average, the FD of a positive competence rating increases by 0.06 if the voter-party distance is large (4 on an 11-point scale). An explanation for this might be that voters already have a high probability to support an ideologically close party. In such cases, competence can hardly boost the chances to support the party any further. On the other hand, party support is generally low if the voter does not share the party's position in the political space. In this scenario, competence can make a big difference when it comes to the vote decision. These voters might not fully agree with the position of the party but they acknowledge that it is handling their MIP competently, which in turn increases the expected utility gained from electing the party. The voting probability is systematically lowest, when the ideological distance is large and the party not competent. On average, the voting probability in this

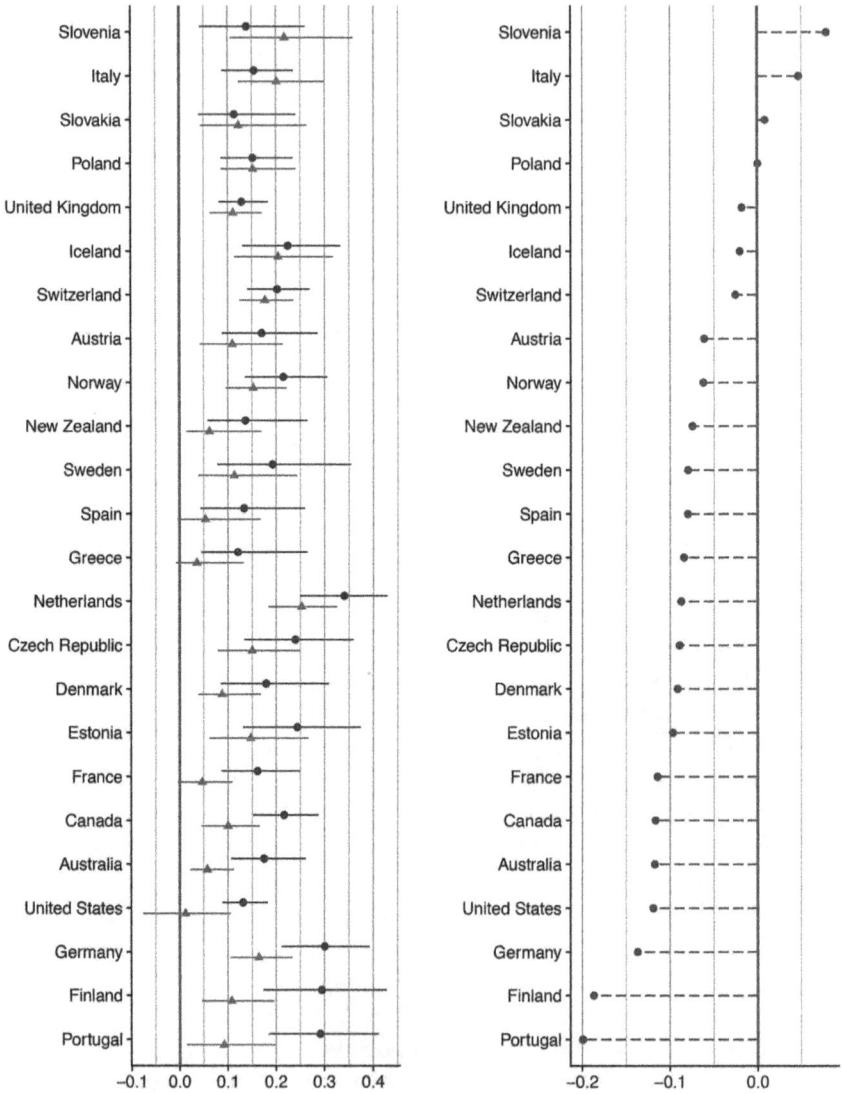

Figure 6.5. First Differences: Interaction Voter-Party Distance. *Sources*: CSES, ParlGov, CMP, and own illustrations.

Note: Left: FDs associated with changing party competence from 'not competent' to 'competent'. Round markers = large voter-party distance; triangle markers = small voter-party distance. Whiskers = 95 per cent HPDs. Right: Difference between the two voter types. Negative values indicate that the FDs are larger for voters with a large voter-party distance.

scenario amounts to 0.58. In this situation, a positive competence evaluation has a strong impact on the vote and is often able to compensate for the lack of ideological proximity. Across all countries, the probability to support a party increases by 0.19 on average when competence ratings are positive, despite the ideological differences. However, if the ideological distance is small, the average voting probability is high, even when the party is not competent (0.71 on average). With such strong issue preferences, competence adds little to the voting probability (average FD of 0.12). From a party perspective, competence is only the cherry on top of the cake.

6.4 CONCLUSION

Until this day, the Downsian proximity model is the most important representative of the issue voting theory. The approach paints the picture of a well-informed citizen, who is represented by a point in a political space. Driven by utility maximization, this voter selects the party located closest to her. In a seminal article, Stokes (1963) provided an influential critique of the spatial rational. He observed that many issues are characterized by agreement. On these so-called valence issues, the machinery of spatial voting does not work. In this case, performance or competence evaluations take over the role of voter-party proximity as the main driver of the vote choice. Competence-based voting bridges these two models (De Sio and Weber 2014). In the theoretical framework, I have argued that issue ownership voters follow three assumptions (section 3.2.1): First, issue ownership voters derive utility from having an issue handled by competent party. Second, they base their evaluations of party competence on multiple sources. Third, a voter's evaluation of competence is more crucial, when it concerns an important political topic.

Based on this, I postulate a hypothesis according to which considering a party best at handling the MIP increases the probability to support the party at the ballot box (H5). The analysis lends strong support for this claim in all countries. The baseline model suggests that competence boosts the voting probability between 0.3 (United States) and 0.6 (Slovakia). However, once I introduce party issue attention, party performance, voter-party distance, and partisanship to the models, the impact of competence decreases. On average, the FDs drop by 0.26, compared to the baseline model. This again draws our attention to the fact that competence evaluations share important variance with other explanations of the vote choice, most importantly partisanship. However, even with these strong controls, the increase in predicted probability associated with a change of party competence remains credible and strong. A full model estimating the effect of competence across all twenty-four countries confirms that, on average, the probability to support a party increases by 0.17 as competence switches from 'not competent' to 'competent'.

I further find that voter-party distance and partisanship moderate competence-based voting. Partisans and, to a lesser extent, voters who share the same ideology as the party in question, less often base their voting decisions on competence. This shows that the effect of competence is not uniform across the entire electorate. However, especially with regard to ideological proximity, the results need further testing. Instead of measuring the moderating effect of the ideological position (on the left-right axis), it would be important to analyse how the voter-party distance on the MIP moderates issue competence.

The results presented in this chapter have several important implications. First, party competence perceptions are a universal driver of the vote choice. Issue ownership voting has an independent effect on the vote, which other factors cannot substitute. The chapter highlights that, regardless of the election, competence helps improving our understanding of the electoral decision beyond what we know from other models of voting. While previous studies have arrived at a similar conclusion, the present analysis enters uncharted territory with regard to the number of countries included and its focus on the actual vote choice in national legislative elections as outcome variable. Second, to some extent, party competence, partisanship, voter-party distance, party performance, and issue attention explain the same variance of the voting preferences. This is an unsurprising finding, given that chapter 5 has shown the close relationship between competence and these concepts. Third, from a party perspective, being competent pays large electoral dividends. Whenever possible, party strategists should spare no effort to gain ownership by adjusting their issue attention, or by highlighting their performance record on an issue (or highlighting the poor record of an adversary party). Finally, competence-based voting is especially important among nonpartisans and citizens who do not share the same ideology as the party in question. This sheds light on how citizens can compensate a lack of party attachment when making an electoral decision.

Chapter 7

Issue Ownership Voting
across Contexts

When our most important issue is the debt that we're piling on our children and grandchildren, I think it's pretty helpful to have someone in the US Senate who has actually managed billions of dollars and knows how to cut billions of dollars.
Carly Fiorina, Interview in *Your World with Neil Cavuto*, 18 June 2010

The previous chapter has revealed that an individual's assessment of how competently a party handles an issue stems from different sources and has a strong impact on his or her electoral decision. Voters are more likely to support a party if they think it is best at handling the MIP on the agenda. In the following, I analyse the role of party system polarization, party system fragmentation, and the clarity of responsibility in issue ownership voting. Several contributions have pointed out that issue voting varies depending on the political environment. This research is mostly on proximity voting (e.g. Alvarez and Nagler 2004; Brody and Page 1972; Kroh 2003), economic voting (e.g. Powell and Whitten 1993), or performance voting (e.g. Giger 2011). The question whether contextual settings moderate competence-based voting has received very little attention so far. In light of this, it is a necessary next step to introduce the political environment to issue ownership voting theory. The fact that the few existing studies have produced ambiguous findings (see Green and Hobolt 2008; Kuechler 1991; Lachat 2011; Pardos-Prado 2012) makes this an even more relevant research topic.

Given the less than clear-cut theoretical expectations, I propose conflicting hypotheses on polarization and fragmentation (sections 3.3.1 and 3.3.2). I further expect that issue ownership voting increases with high levels of clarity of responsibility. As this chapter will demonstrate, issue ownership voting is slightly stronger the more fragmented a party system. However, the findings do not support the view that polarization or clarity of responsibility shape competence-based voting. In general, I do not find a setting, in which issue ownership voting is not an important driver of the vote choice. This underscores the universal importance of the approach.

7.1 METHOD

I test the hypotheses with individual-level data from the CSES. Country-level and party-level data come from the ParlGov database and the CPDS. I measure party issue attention with the CMP.

The analysis is split into three parts. I start by replicating the first comparative analysis on the impact of competence in elections (Kuechler 1991). While I am able to reproduce the original findings, I also detect flaws in the measurement strategy. These problems are pivotal as they yield unreliable findings (especially with regard to fragmentation). To remedy this, I use the differences in predicted probabilities from the full issue ownership voting model (chapter 6) and plot them against party system polarization, fragmentation, and clarity of responsibility. This will give us a first idea of how competence-based voting interacts with contextual settings. I then turn to hybrid regression models with different country samples. The outcome in this analysis is the vote choice. This nominal variable has between two and seven categories depending on the effective number of parties ($j = 1, \ldots, J$) in the country (for the full list of parties, see table 4.3). Inputs vary either across voters $i = 1, \ldots, n$ (x_i), or across individuals and parties (x_{ij}). Variables of the former type are the respondent's age, sex, gender, education, political sophistication and the MIP. I introduce these covariates in sections 4.2.1 and 4.2.5. The second type of input is a matrix where the number of columns corresponds to the number of parties in the country.[1] This concerns the main predictor 'competence evaluation', as well as the covariates 'voter-party distance', 'partisanship', 'performance', and 'issue attention' (see sections 4.2.2, 4.2.3, and 4.2.4). In the case of 'competence evaluation', cell a_{ij} takes the value 1 if the voter considers party j is best able to handle the MIP. All other cells ($a_ik, \forall k \neq j$) of the voter are 0 (i.e. not competent). Since I estimate models across several democracies, indicators are additionally indexed for country ($c = 1, \ldots, C$). The systematic part of the model is specified as follows (equation 7.1):

$$V_{ijc} = \beta_{0jc} + \beta_{1jc} \cdot \text{age}_{ic} + \beta_{2jc} \cdot \text{sex}_{ic} + \beta_{3jc} \cdot \text{education}_{ic}$$
$$+ \beta_{4jc} \cdot \text{sophistication}_{ic} + \beta_{5jc} \cdot \text{social}_{ic} + \beta_{6jc} \cdot \text{external}_{ic} + \beta_{7jc} \cdot \text{services}_{ic}$$
$$+ \beta_{8jc} \cdot \text{immigration}_{ic} + \beta_{9jc} \cdot \text{quality}_{ic} + \beta_{10jc} \cdot \text{other}_{ic} + \beta_{11jc} \cdot \text{security}_{ic} \quad (7.1)$$
$$+ \gamma_1 \cdot \text{competence}_{ijc} + \gamma_2 \cdot \text{partisan}_{ijc} + \gamma_3 \cdot \text{distance}_{ijc}$$
$$+ \gamma_4 \cdot \text{performance}_{ijc} + \gamma_5 \cdot \text{attention}_{ijc}$$

where each voter-specific variable yields $J \cdot C$ parameters (this equals the total number of parties in the analysis). The β_{5jc} to β_{11jc} estimate the effect of the MIP dummies (economy is the reference category). The model picks up five γ parameters, one for each party-specific input. To test hypotheses H8a/b, H9a/b, and H10, I run split-sample regressions for countries with high/low levels of fragmentation, polarization, and clarity of responsibility. This results in a total of six separate models.[2] I implement the models in a Bayesian framework and use the package rjags for R for the estimations and specify uninformative N $(0,10^2)$ priors for all parameters (γ and β).

7.2 BACK TO THE ROOTS: THE CONTEXT OF MATCHING VOTE CHOICE

In 1991, Kuechler argued that high levels of party system fragmentation reinforce the relationship between competence and the vote. For almost two decades, this remained the only systematic issue ownership voting study dealing with the context. Due to the pathbreaking character of the analysis, I propose to replicate these findings with my data and see if I arrive at similar conclusions. However, I will also highlight critical flaws in the analysis. In section 7.3, I then turn to two alternative strategies of analysing contextual effects.

Kuechler measured the impact of party competence in the decision-making process by splitting the electorate in two groups. In the first group, voters cast their ballot for the party they rate best at handling the MIP. Kuechler calls this a "matching vote choice" (1991: 95). In the second group, voters do not support the most competent party on the MIP. Following the original argument, the political environment partially explains the country-level variation of matching voting.

In line with Kuechler, I find that this matching voting varies across the countries in my sample. Whereas the share of matching voters is only 45 per cent in Slovenia, it amounts to 79 per cent in Spain. The remaining countries spread out evenly between these extreme cases. The question is whether we can explain this variation with the political context, as Kuechler suggests. Figure 7.1 plots a country's share of matching voters against party system fragmentation (top panel), polarization (middle panel), and clarity of responsibility (bottom panel). The top panel shows that, as the *number of effective parties* increases (x axis), the share of matching voters decreases (y axis). The effect is substantial. As we move from the lowest observed effective number of parties (2, United States) to the highest observed score (7, the Netherlands), the predicted level of matching voting decreases by 32 percentage points. This lends support for Kuechler's claim that when the number of parties is high, voters perceive parties as close or even identical. In such

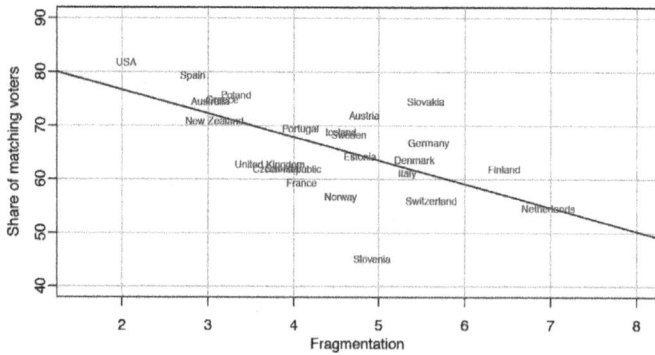

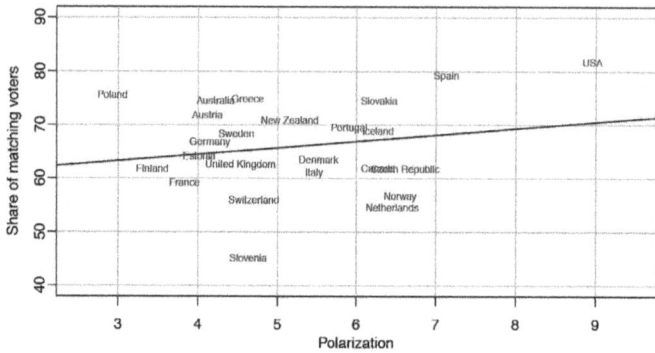

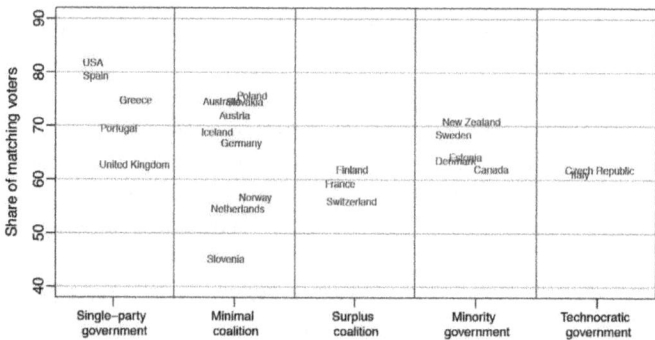

Figure 7.1. Matching Voting Across Contexts. *Source:* CSES and own illustrations.

Note: Grey line = ordinary least squares (OLS) regression line.

situations, voters find it more difficult to match their perceptions of party competence with their vote choice. The middle panel in figure 7.1 shows the relationship between *party system polarization* and matching voting. No clear pattern seems to emerge from this analysis. The grey OLS regression line has a positive slope, but the effect is negligible and mostly driven by the United States. Finally, the bottom panel splits the countries into five different types of government. Following Powell (2000), the *clarity of responsibility* is the highest in single-party majority governments and the lowest in minority or technocratic governments. As it turns out, the link between matching voting and clarity of responsibility is not clear-cut. Countries with single-party majority governments have higher shares of matching voters than countries with other types of government. However, in most categories, the cases are spread out along the y axis. For instance, the share of matching voting in minimal coalition systems ranges from 45 per cent (Slovenia) to 76 per cent (Poland).

7.3 TWO DIFFERENT APPROACHES TO MEASURING THE ROLE OF THE CONTEXT IN ISSUE OWNERSHIP

At first sight, this analysis might be a worthwhile test for contingent contextual effects on issue ownership voting. The variable 'matching vote choice' is easy to grasp and facilitates comparative research since it collapses the relationship between two nominal indicators ('vote choice' and 'party competence') into a single binary measurement. However, a matching vote choice does not mean that the voters actually *base* their decision on competence evaluations or that such evaluations have any impact on the final vote. In fact, this strategy of measuring issue ownership voting produces highly misleading findings. As the matching vote choice combines outcome ('vote choice') and input ('party competence'), we no longer control for confounding variables and therefore overestimate the effect of competence on the vote. Consider the visualization of the FDs in the previous chapter (figure 6.2). In Greece, Spain, or Slovakia, the impact of competence decreases sharply once I control for partisanship voting, proximity voting, and performance voting. In these cases, a fair share of what competence ratings explain in the baseline model is linked to other decision-making strategies. Strikingly, matching voting is highest in the countries where the difference between the baseline model and the full model is the most pronounced. In countries where the effect of competence on the vote is strong and independent, matching voting seems low (the Netherlands and Norway). This suggests that matching voters often do not base their decision on competence and that the variable is a poor measurement for issue ownership voting.

In the following, I propose two different approaches to test the contextual hypotheses. Before introducing the hybrid regression models, I use the differences in predicted probabilities from the previous chapter as indicators for the strength of issue ownership voting and plot them against the contextual variables. The FDs show how much the probability of voting for a party increases when party competence evaluation changes from 'not competent' to 'competent'. The models on which these values are based control for partisanship, voter-party distance, performance, issue attention, and several sociodemographic variables.

Figure 7.2 shows the magnitude of issue ownership voting across varying levels of *party system fragmentation.* H8a claims that as the effective number of parties increase, elections became more competitive. This renders the electoral base of the party more homogeneous, which allows parties to express their positions more freely without singling out potential voters. Following Lachat (2011), this should ease issue voting. H8b postulates an opposite effect according to which fragmented party systems are highly complex and therefore dampen the role of issues in the decision-making process (Kroh 2009). Whether this claim extends to issue ownership voting has not been tested. My analysis lends support to H8a. I find that the importance of competence in elections grows as the effective number of parties increases. The magnitude of this effect is striking. As we move from the country with the least fragmented party system (the United States) to the country with the most fragmented system (the Netherlands), the predicted FD increases by 0.16.[3] Note that this result is fundamentally different than the one based on the matching voting analysis.

Let me now address the role of *party system polarization* in individual-level issue ownership. Figure 7.3 shows how the extent of issue ownership voting varies across different levels of party system polarization. H9a postulates that polarization decreases issue ownership voting as campaigns in such settings are not fought over valence issues (trade-off hypothesis). H9b posits that competence ratings have a stronger effect if parties take ideologically distinct positions. In polarized systems, party competence is more accessible and thus more likely to determine the vote choice. I do not find empirical support for either of these claims. The visualization shows that in countries with entirely different levels of party system polarization (e.g. Poland and the United States), issue ownership can have almost the same effect. In a similar vein, issue ownership voting might be much stronger in one country than in another, even though the level of polarization is almost identical (e.g. the Netherlands and Slovakia). This demonstrates that issue ownership voting takes place regardless of how distinct party positions are.[4]

In a last step, I turn to the relationship between the *clarity of responsibility* and issue ownership voting. Figure 7.4 shows the five conditions of government. In H10, I expect issue ownership voting to be strongest in systems with

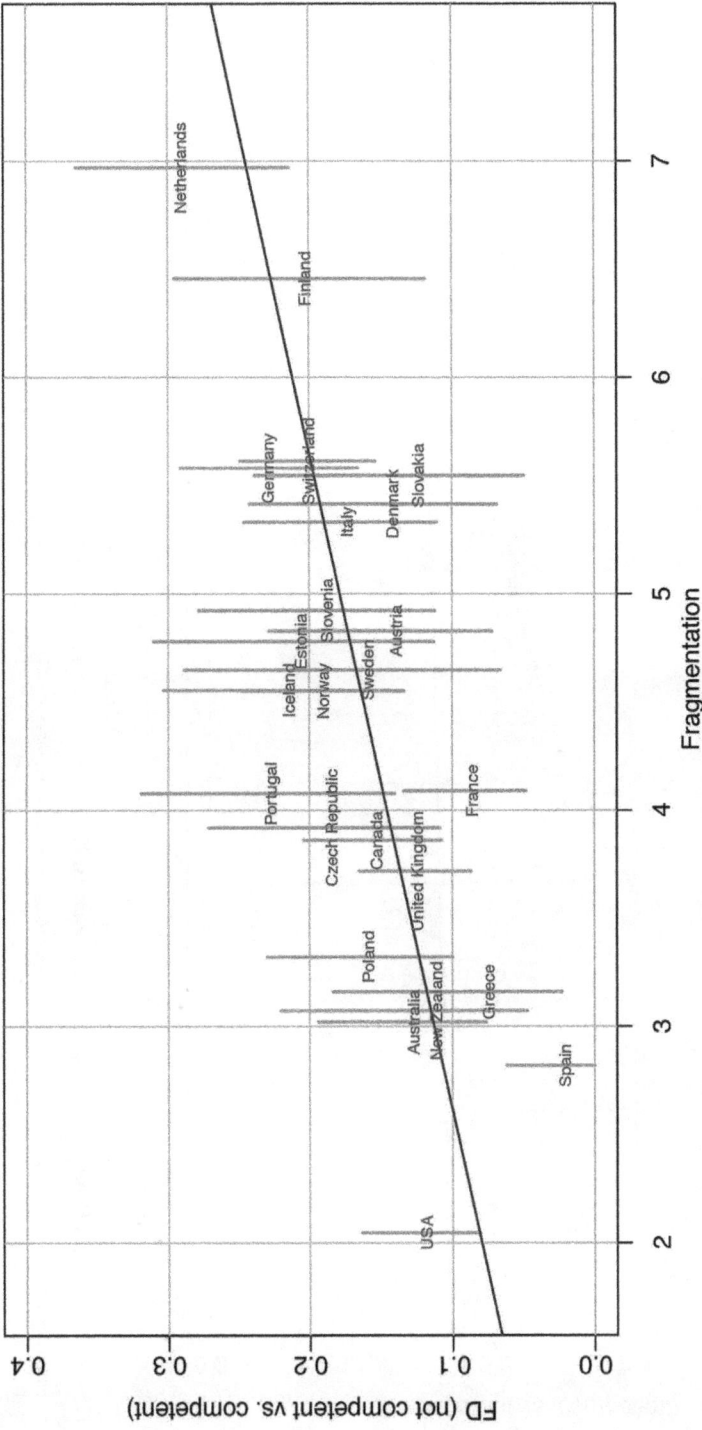

Figure 7.2. Predicted Vote Choice: Fragmentation. *Sources:* CSES, ParlGov, CMP, and own illustration.

Note: FDs from the full issue ownership voting model (figure 6.2). Whiskers = 95 per cent HPDs. Grey line = OLS regression line.

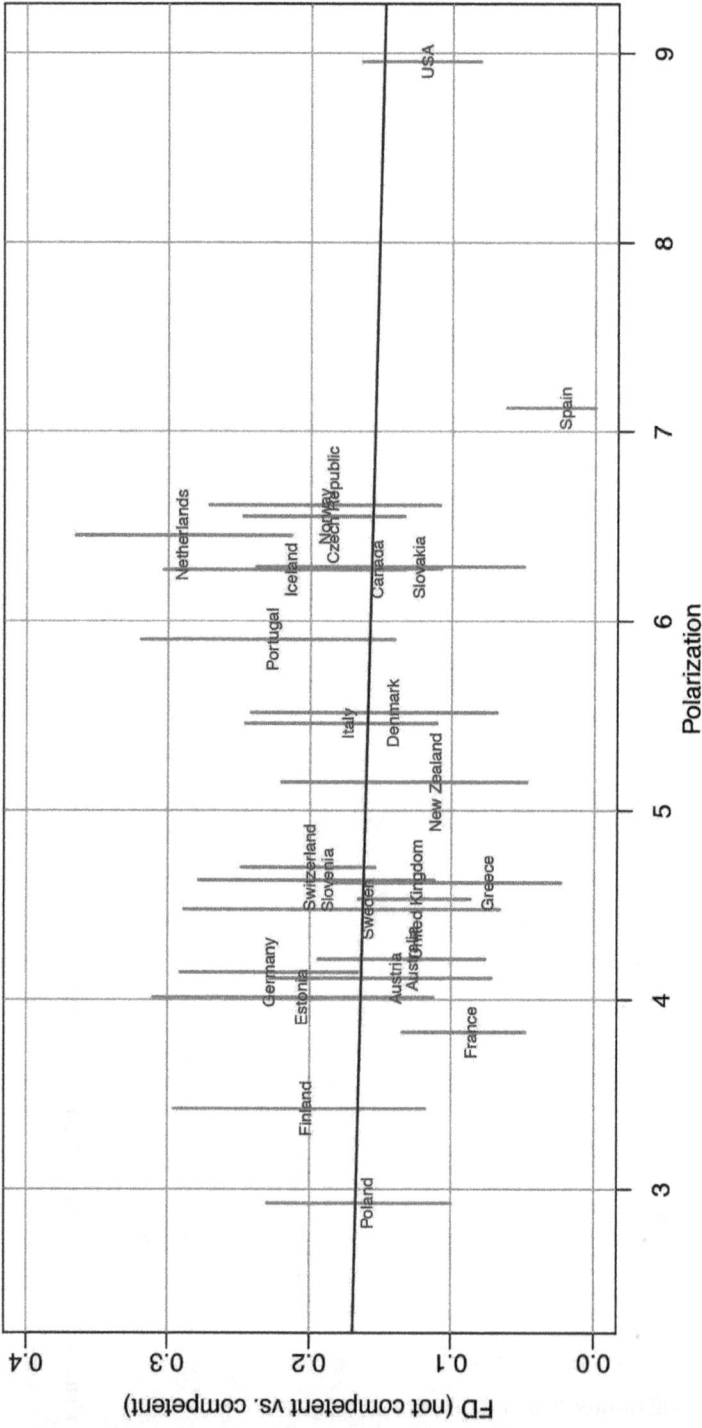

Figure 7.3. Predicted Vote Choice: Polarization. *Sources: CSES, ParlGov, CMP, and own illustration.*

Note: FDs from the full issue ownership voting model (figure 6.2). Whiskers = 95 per cent HPDs. Grey line = OLS regression line.

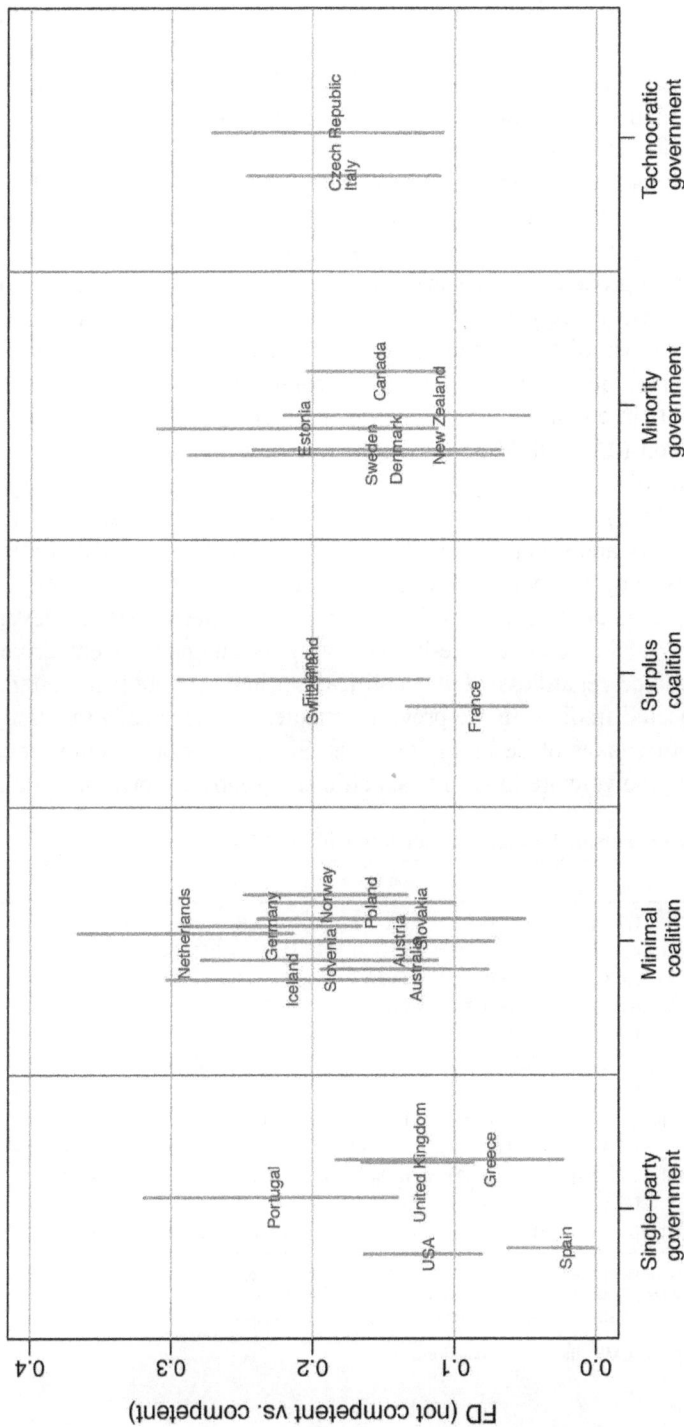

Figure 7.4. Predicted Vote Choice: Clarity of Responsibility. *Sources:* CSES, ParlGov, CMP, **and own illustration.**

Note: FDs from the full issue ownership voting model (see figure 6.2). Whiskers = 95 per cent HPDs. Average FDs: single-party government = 0.11, minimal coalition = 0.18, surplus coalition = 0.16, minority government = 0.16, technocratic government = 0.18.

single-party majority governments and weakest in countries with technocratic governments. The analysis shows high levels of variation within most categories. For example, in the category 'single-party governments', FDs range between 0.02 and 0.22. Democracies with minimal coalition governments tend to see higher levels of competence-based voting, but generally, the FDs are spread out, too. No systematic pattern emerges from the analysis, which questions the view that high-clarity countries see higher levels of competence-based voting than low-clarity systems.

The second approach for measuring contextual effects is based on the regression models in equation 7.1. These models estimate competence-based voting across different country samples. Table 7.1 summarizes all party-specific parameters in six different environments. Rows two and three show the results in countries with above-average and below-average levels of fragmentation (M_{1a} and M_{1b}). The models in row four and five present effects in high polarized party systems (M_{2a}) and systems with low ideological dispersion (M_{2b}). The models for low and high clarity of responsibility appear in rows six and seven (M_{3a} and M_{3b}). The HPDs indicate that predictors are positive/negative when they span only positive/negative values.

All γ_1 parameters are positive and highly credible on the 95 per cent level. This underscores that competence-based voting is an independent driver of the vote choice regardless of the political setting. Although important, this is an expected finding. In the previous chapter, we have seen that issue ownership voting takes place in all countries. Situations where competence is not affecting the vote are limited to specific subgroups of voters in certain

Table 7.1. Issue Ownership Voting: Full Model in Different Contexts

Country	Comp., γ_1	Emph., γ_2	Perf., γ_3	PI, γ_4	Dist., γ_5	Cont.
M_{1a} low frag.	1.11	0.00	0.15	1.81	−0.20	✓
	[1.04, 1.17]	[−0.01, 0.01]	[0.10, 0.19]	[1.73, 1.88]	[−0.22, −0.18]	
M_{1b} high frag.	1.43	−0.01	0.13	2.32	−0.20	✓
	[1.36, 1.50]	[−0.05, 0.03]	[0.07, 0.19]	[2.24, 2.40]	[−0.22, −0.18]	
M_{2a} low polar.	1.17	0.01	0.18	1.98	−0.17	✓
	[1.10, 1.23]	[−0.04, 0.05]	[0.13, 0.22]	[1.91, 2.05]	[−0.19, −0.15]	
M_{2b} high polar.	1.38	0.01	0.08	2.17	−0.25	✓
	[1.31, 1.45]	[0.00, 0.03]	[0.02, 0.14]	[2.09, 2.25]	[−0.27, −0.23]	
M_{3a} low clarity	1.18	0.01	0.02	2.17	−0.21	✓
	[1.11, 1.25]	[0.00, 0.01]	[−0.04, 0.08]	[2.09, 2.25]	[−0.23, −0.18]	
M_{3b} high clarity	1.33	0.01	0.20	1.98	−0.20	✓
	[1.26, 1.39]	[0.00, 0.03]	[0.16, 0.25]	[1.91, 2.05]	[−0.22, −0.18]	

Note: Marginal posterior densities of γ (equation 7.1). Numbers in brackets are 95 per cent HPD. MCMC with 150,000 it. after 50,000 it. burn-in. Comp. = competence, emph. = party issue emphasis, perf. = government performance, dist. = voter-party distance, PI = party identification, cont. = control variables.

Sources: CSES, ParlGov, CMP, and own calculations.

countries (e.g. nonpartisans in the United States). The regression table, moreover, confirms that voters are less probable to support positionally distant parties (γ_5) and more probable to vote for a party they feel attached to (γ_4). As we would expect from previous research, performance (γ_3) does not have a credible effect on the vote if clarity of responsibility is low. Finally, parties that put a lot of emphasis on the voters' MIP do not get additional support at the ballot box (γ_2).

The observation that issue ownership voting takes place in all contexts does not mean that the extent to which people use their competence evaluation to form a decision is the same everywhere. To assess if the strength of competence-based voting is contingent on the political setting, I turn to graphical presentation of the regressions. Figure 7.5 shows a respondent's predicted probability to support the party he or she voted for, given his or her observed profile, in countries with low (top panel) and high (bottom panel) fragmentation. Each panel simulates six conditions. The first two markers from the left show the impact of party competence rating on the vote ('party not competent' versus 'party competent'). The second and third markers depict a decrease in voter-party distance (from 4 to 0 points). The fifth and sixth markers show probabilities for nonpartisans and partisans. The FDs indicate the difference between two markers.

In countries with low levels of *party system fragmentation*, a positive competence evaluation increases the probability to support the party by 0.14. This value increases to 0.20 when many parties compete in an election. This supports the claim that, due to their homogeneous electorate, parties can express their issue preferences and competences more freely in fragmented systems. In such settings, voters acknowledge issue-handling competence and tend to base their vote choice on such evaluations (H8a). I do not find that voters turn away from issue-based voting because fragmented systems impose a high level of complexity to elections (H8b). While fragmentation does not influence the extent of proximity voting, it reinforces partisanship-based voting. This speaks against a trade-off between issue ownership voting and partisanship or proximity voting, at least in the context of party system fragmentation.

When *polarization* is low, the probability to support a party is 0.59 in the 'party not-competent' scenario and 0.76 in the 'party competent' scenario (figure 7.6). The premium associated with a favourable issue competence evaluation is the same in polarized settings. This confirms the findings from the previous section and runs against both polarization hypotheses (H9a and H9b). While proximity voting yields the same effect in both settings, partisanship voting is slightly stronger in the low-polarization context.

Fragmentation low

Fragmentation high

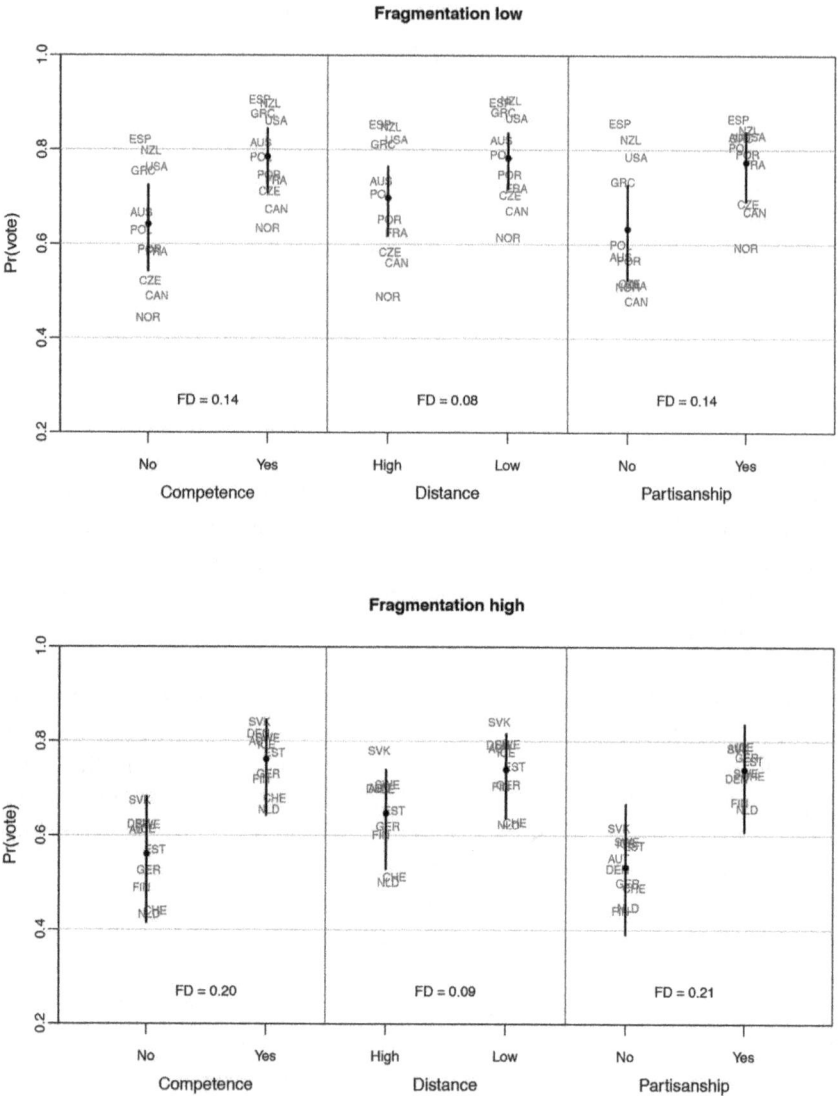

Figure 7.5. Decision-Making Strategies and Fragmentation. *Sources*: CSES, ParlGov, CMP, and own illustrations.

Note: FDs from the split-sample issue ownership voting models (see table 7.1). Whiskers = 95 per cent HPDs.

This supports Lachat (2011), who argues that voters should rely less on the partisan heuristic when elections are competitive.

Figure 7.7 visualizes the results for *clarity of responsibility*. For this analysis, I regroup countries with a single-party and a minimal coalition into the category 'high clarity'. The remaining conditions of government composition

Polarization low

Polarization high

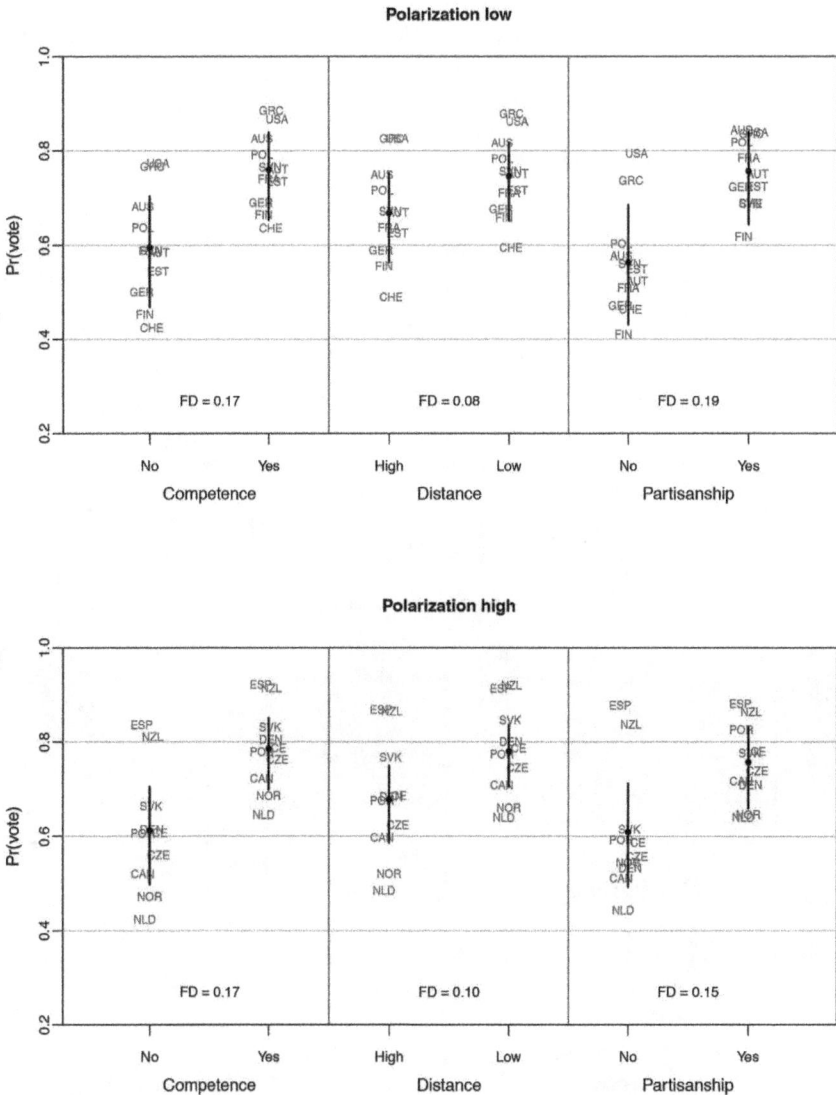

Figure 7.6. Decision-Making Strategies and Polarization. *Sources*: CSES, ParlGov, CMP, and own illustrations.

Note: FDs from the split-sample issue ownership voting models (see table 7.1). Whiskers = 95 per cent HPDs.

(surplus coalition, minority government, technocratic government) constitute the group of countries with low clarity. The picture is largely the same in both settings. In contrast to my assumption in H10, the extent to which voters can attribute responsibility for a specific political outcome does not condition competence-based voting. In fact, clarity of responsibility does not moderate

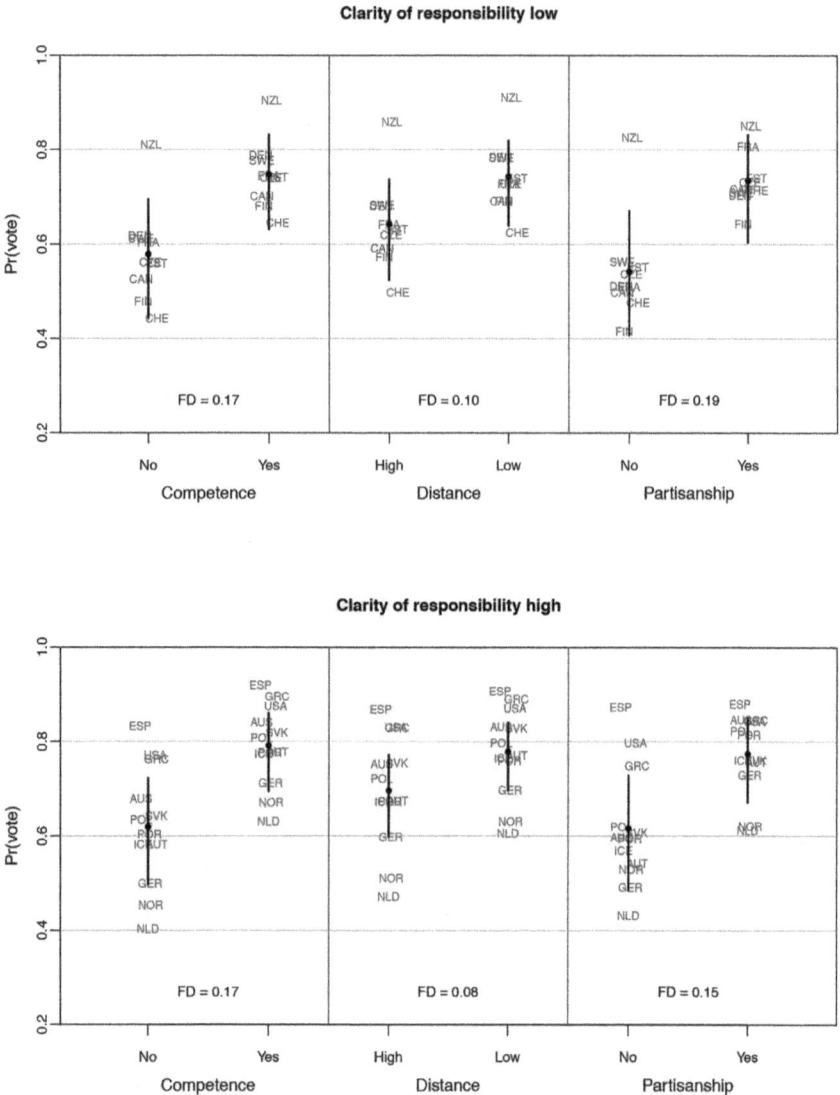

Figure 7.7. Decision-Making Strategies and Clarity of Responsibility. *Sources:* **CSES, ParlGov, CMP, and own illustrations.**

Note: FDs from the split-sample issue ownership voting models (see table 7.1). Whiskers = 95 per cent HPDs.

any of the three voting strategies. One could argue that this disappointing finding is due to the crude separation of the countries in low-and high-clarity cases. However, such binary measurements are not new to the literature on clarity of responsibility (Giger 2011). Moreover, the results mirror those in the previous section, where I examine five conditions of government.

7.4 CONCLUSION

This chapter has investigated the conditioning effects of party system polarization, fragmentation, and the clarity of responsibility on issue ownership voting. Thus far, the role of the context in competence-based voting has received little scholarly attention. The few existing studies have come to conflicting conclusions.

Lachat (2011) argues that as *fragmentation* increases, individual parties appeal to a smaller number of voters and thus present a clearer image of their position and competences. Fragmentation should thus boost issue ownership voting (H8a). This is contrasted by research on proximity voting, where a negative moderating effect of fragmentation on issue voting is assumed. The idea is that fragmentation increases party system complexity and that in such environments, voters find it difficult to evaluate party positions and act on issue perceptions (see also Kuechler 1991). If proximity voting and issue ownership voting follow the same dynamics, fragmentation should decrease issue ownership voting (H8b). On *polarization*, the debate is structured along different lines. A first group of researchers advocates a negative contingent effect of party system *polarization* on competence-based voting (H9a). In polarized systems, they argue, campaigns are fought over position issues, which, in turn, increases proximity voting and dampens issue ownership voting. A second group of scholars claiming that polarization increases all aspects of party competition, including issue competence, challenges this view. That is, polarization should increase the effects of competence ratings on the vote (H9b). Finally, I analyse how *clarity of responsibility* shapes competence-based voting. Thus far, no study has linked these two strands of literature, which makes this an exploratory analysis. In the theoretical framework, I presume that when it is difficult for citizens to attribute responsibility to political parties, it should also be difficult to evaluate issue-handling competence and, ultimately, act on such perceptions. I, thus, postulate that high clarity of responsibility should increase issue ownership voting (H10).

In a first step, I analyse if the contextual setting explains the varying FDs from the full issue ownership voting model (section 6.2). I find that party competence has a stronger effect on the vote in highly fragmented systems (e.g. the Netherlands or Finland). In Spain, the United States, or Greece, competence-based voting is less important. This finding bolsters the idea that parties have a clear profile when their electorate is small and homogeneous. In this situation, competence becomes more readily available as a decision-making criterion. A split-sample regression analysis confirms this result. In countries with low effective number of parties, a party's premium for being competent is lower than in countries with many parties. The other two contextual factors have no clear impact on issue ownership voting. On the reasons for that, we can only speculate. With regard to polarization, the claims in H9a and H9b might cancel each other out. On the one hand, systems with ideologically distinct parties might render competence evaluations more easily available. On the other hand, such systems might also foster debates on the positional rather than the valence component of an issue. Clarity of responsibility, too, does not affect issue ownership voting. However, this does not necessarily mean that it is not important for individual-level issue ownership. A cursory analysis has hinted that clarity of responsibility is low in the three countries, where performance has no impact on party competence (chapter 5). Put differently, clarity might not moderate the effect of competence but might influence how such evaluations emerge.

The analysis has further revealed that the share of voters supporting the best party on the MIP is not a good instrument to measure competence-based voting. Matching voting is highest in countries where controlling for partisanship and voter-party distance dampens the effect of competence the most. Since the matching vote choice has not established itself as measurement for issue ownership voting, this one could see this as a minor finding. Nevertheless, Kuechler's study has a pioneering character with regard to comparative research on issue ownership voting. Therefore, it is crucial to understand the results and, more importantly, why they might be flawed. Second, the analysis underscores how crucial controlling for other determinants of the vote choice can be. Effects of baseline models are correlated with the matching vote choice and should not be used as indicators for the strength of issue ownership voting.

The take-home message of this chapter is threefold. First, issue ownership voting as defined in this project is not the same thing as supporting the most competent party. It is about the effect of competence evaluations on the vote choice approximated in fully specified models. Second, competence-based voting takes place in all kinds of contexts. I do not find a single setting where competence has no credible effect on how citizens make their decision. This speaks for the universal importance of individual-level issue ownership in national elections. Third, fragmented party systems reinforce issue ownership voting. In such settings, parties can strengthen their profile because they often cater to a small, homogeneous electoral base.

Chapter 8

General Conclusion

This study is about the origins and consequences of party issue competence. It shows that individual-level issue ownership is a multifaceted concept and that voters want competent parties handling the issues they care about. The effect of competence is strong and especially pronounced among nonpartisans. Fragmented systems tend to foster issue ownership voting. The study, moreover, provides a unique methodological framework to analyse decision-making in a large number of legislative elections. It brings a comparative approach to a largely national literature.

In the following, I review the contributions of the study and highlight their implications for the democratic process (section 8.1). I then turn to the limitations of the analysis and point out future research avenues (section 8.2).

8.1 GENERAL FINDINGS AND IMPLICATIONS OF THE STUDY

Chapter 5 postulates a fresh view on the determinants of individual-level issue ownership (research question 1). It demonstrates that perceptions of competence are derived from multiple factors, some of which parties can manipulate in the short run.

The analysis does not support the idea that parties generally build up reputations on issues simply "by *emphasising certain topics* more than others" (Budge 2015: 761). I do find that parties can use their manifesto to shape their ownership in two-thirds of the countries. However, in half of these cases, the observed effects are substantially weak. Parties must vastly shift their attention towards an issue, in order to gain only little ownership. In the remaining countries, above-average issue attention does not yield credible effects on competence at all. Presumably, party manifestos are not a good channel for signalling shifts of issue attention to voters. They indicate the importance a party attaches to an issue (Klingemann et al. 2006), but if the media does not pick up these changes in the reporting, voters will hardly ever take notice of them. In most countries, competence is linked to *government performance*. Parties are more likely to be rated best at handling the MIP, when they perform well in office. This is an important result, as it shows that competence is not just the product of programmatic expectations or promises in the manifesto. It is also tied to the quality of the policy output. I further show that *ideological considerations* feed into citizens' evaluations of competence. This qualifies claims from early studies in the field, according to which position and competence are fully independent from each other. Finally, the 'perceptual screen' of *partisanship* affects the way voters attribute competence to parties. The theory of partisan-motivated reasoning might provide the psychological underpinning of this effect. In this view, voters use their party attachment as anchor from which they derive other preferences such as competence.

In chapter 6, I investigate "issue ownership voting" (Petrocik 1996: 833) or "competence-based voting" (Green 2007: 646) in twenty-four national elections (research question 2). This type of voting is part of the rational choice framework and hypothesizes that *voters support the most competent party on the most important issue*. My analysis bolsters the issue ownership voting hypothesis in every country. On average, a voter's probability to support a party increases by 0.17, if he or she thinks that it is best at handling the top issue on his or her agenda. In terms of size, this effect matches the one associated with partisanship. All results control for partisanship voting, proximity voting, and performance voting. This means that issue ownership furthers our understanding of electoral decision-making beyond what we know from these approaches. A refined version of the model reveals moderating effects of partisanship and voter-party distance. In most elections, competence-based voting is stronger if the voter-party distance is large. Hence, voters are willing to support a party, when they think it will handle their MIP well, in spite of ideological differences. In addition, competence considerations are much more important for nonpartisans than for partisans. The latter are already likely to support their party, even when they do not think that it handles their MIP especially well. In contrast, nonpartisans have to rely on substantial decision-making strategies such as competence voting since they cannot, per definition, base their vote choice on the partisan heuristic.

Chapter 7 delves deeper into the cross-national differences of issue ownership voting (research question 3). I replicate the first comparative analysis on competence-based voting with my own data. While the results are similar to the original study by Kuechler (1991), the analysis reveals serious flaws in the methodological approach. Therefore, I propose two alternative strategies to measure the moderating effects of the context on issue ownership voting, both of which yield similar results. Neither points to the conclusion that party system polarization or clarity of responsibly account for variation in issue ownership voting. However, citizens are more likely to base their decision on competence if the effective number of parties competing in an election is high. This stands in stark contrast to Kuechler's study where fragmentation dampens competence-based voting. The results, moreover, speak against previous findings, showing that polarization and competence-based voting are positively (Lachat 2011; Pardos-Prado 2012) or negatively (Green and Hobolt 2008) related. More importantly, though, the analysis confirms that issue ownership is a universal driver of the vote choice in all types of political systems.

The contribution of this project is not limited to these findings. The study develops a comprehensive theoretical framework in a sometimes astonishingly undertheorized field of research. It further proposes a methodological approach to investigate competence-based voting in a large number of national legislative elections. Thus far, comparative research has measured issue ownership voting either with flawed indicators or with the PTV variable. The highly flexible hybrid regression models used in this analysis overcome the problem of not being able to simultaneously measure effects of party-specific and voter-specific variables (van der Brug 2004). At the same time, I sidestep running hierarchical logistic regressions on a stacked dataset, a strategy that would likely produce flawed results. Furthermore, the study expands the narrow focus of issue ownership voting research on a handful of Western European countries. It includes twenty-four democracies, in many of which issue ownership voting has never been tested in the context of national elections. This approach increases our confidence in proclaiming competence a universal and important driver of the vote choice. Additionally, by analysing a large number of countries, I can tackle a further shortcoming of the current literature, namely the near-absence of contextual variables. The study shows a moderating effect of party system fragmentation and thus underlines the potential of systematic variables in explaining variation of issue ownership voting.

The study has multiple implications for electoral research and, more generally, party competition in advanced democratic systems. First, it emphasizes the role of competence in the decision-making. It is fair to say that all models of the vote choice improve, if they include measures for party competence. This suggests that there is no substitute for competence in elections. Essentially, this is good news for the democratic process. As Dalton (1984: 282) puts it, issue voting can make "candidates more responsive to public opinion". Adams, Merrill, and Grofman (2005) argue that political systems, where a critical share of the electorate follows the logic of issue voting, tend to produce governments and parliaments that express the collective policy preference of the people. Therefore, issue voting can be seen as a crucial element of political representation. According to Powell (2004), the congruence between voters and legislators is an important indicator for the quality of a political system. The results of this project are of particular importance, as issue ownership voting is cognitively less demanding than other forms of issue voting (Lachat 2011). Competence-based voting comes with the aforementioned advantages of issue voting without being the prerogative of the well informed. The findings have, moreover, implications for the way parties compete with each other. Besides pointing out how pivotal competence on an issue can be, the analysis shows how parties can shape their reputation on an issue. In most cases, the electorate rewards good government performance with attributing competence. In one-third of the countries, parties can influence ownership by shifting their attention on an issue.

8.2 LIMITATIONS AND FUTURE RESEARCH AVENUES

The study has several limitations. First, like most nonexperimental studies in public opinion research, I cannot demonstrate a *causal relationship* between concepts. This problem runs through nearly all empirical tests (see the discussion in section 3.4). A second concern regards the question about the MIP. Despite its widespread use in surveys and scientific research, this indicator has been criticized in the past (Jennings and Wlezien 2011; Wlezien 2005). I agree that the salience component of the question can be ambiguous. The respondent might name the problem currently at the top of his or her mind or the problem that is actually salient in the public debate. However, the CSES project tries to tackle this by asking an egocentric and a sociotropic MIP question. Whether the term 'problem' fosters confusion or not is difficult to say. However, Jennings and Wlezien (2011: 554) do not find a systematic difference between questions on the MIP and questions on the most important issue. Third, the study does not include perceived party competence *on issues that are not at the top of the voter's agenda*. This is a key difference to other contributions in the field, where respondents indicate the most competent parties on a series of issues. The advantage of the MIP/competence variable is that it reflects "the natural connection" (Bélanger and Meguid 2008: 479) between salience and competence. However, other studies have demonstrated that competence on more than just one issue influence the voting decision (e.g. Lachat 2014; Lutz and Sciarini 2016). Focusing only on the effect of a single issue, even when it is the most important, might not provide a full account of competence-based voting. Presumably, competence evaluations on non-MIP issues further impact electoral decision-making. In other words, this study likely underestimates the overall role of issue competence assessments in the voting process.

Measuring competence ratings on multiple issues is a promising development. Nevertheless, compared to this strategy, the MIP/competence combination has a few advantages. Due to the predefined issue battery, respondents can feel pressured to identify a competent party on issues they do not care about and/or do not know much about. While political experts might easily identify the most competent party on less well-known issues, many respondents will be overtaxed with such questions. The MIP/competence combination lowers this risk since respondents only have to identify a competent party on an issue they deeply care about. A final limitation is *the wording of the competence question*. A recent survey experiment shows that a similar question is especially affected by voter-party distance and party identification (Walgrave et al. 2016). Unfortunately, almost none of the lately proposed issue ownership questions are available in more than one election study. At this time, using an alternative measurement of competence ownership would render a large comparative study infeasible. Besides this, I do not think that it is a realistic goal to find competence questions that are untainted by partisanship and position. As Walgrave et al. show, all competence issue ownership questions are, to some extent, shaped by positional cues and party identification. I agree, however, that we have to get a better grasp at how these concepts are related to each other.

What is a limitation to this study is an opportunity for future research. Over the past years, we have seen individual-level issue ownership literature developing at a tremendous pace. Since the beginning of this project, many new studies have been published and have widened our understanding of electoral decision-making in democratic societies. Today, we are confident that the voting decision is linked to perceptions of competence. Future attempts will have to carve out conditions that facilitate competence-based voting. In chapter 6, we have seen that competence-based voting varies across the countries in the sample and that party system fragmentation explains parts of this variation. However, we should continue to analyse how other contextual factors moderate issue ownership voting. Presumably, contextual settings affect issue ownership beyond the voting process. For instance, the role of performance as a source of issue ownership could depend on the level of clarity of responsibility in a country. Another open question is how issue ownership voting evolves over time. Given the available data, analysing several elections in the same country is a challenging, but by no means impossible task. In their study, Green and Hobolt (2008) have demonstrated the potential merits of such research. They showed that contextual changes in Great Britain affected the importance of party competence ratings in electoral decision-making. Finally, experimental studies could answer many of the open questions. To some extent, this has already been done to test different survey questions on issue ownership. However, experiments could moreover clarify causal links between different concepts. This would tackle an important limitation of this project and could be a real contribution to the literature.

Notes

1. INTRODUCTION

1. Note that throughout this book, 'competence' denotes a party's perceived ability to handle a political issue. When referring to 'voter competence' (Ashworth and Bueno De Mesquita 2014), I use the terms 'political sophistication' or 'political knowledge'.

2. For single-country studies, see Wagner and Zeglovits (2014) and Stubager and Slothuus (2013).

2. PERSPECTIVES ON ISSUE VOTING AND ISSUE OWNERSHIP VOTING

1. In the following, the terms 'aggregate-level issue ownership' and 'party-level issue ownership' are used interchangeably.

2. For instance, the value dimensions in Kriesi et al. (2008) are the result of a factor analysis with a set of issues on the input side.

3. According to Downs (1957: 6), rationality contains five elements (see also Arrow 1951): (1) When confronted with a choice, rational actors are always able to make a decision. (2) The rational citizen ranks his or her options in order of preference. (3) Preferences are transitive; that is, they can be compared with each other. Imagine a scenario where a voter has to choose between parties *a*, *b*, and *c*. If the voter prefers party *a* to party *b* and party *b* to party *c*, then, following the axiom of transitivity, he or she must also prefer party *a* to party *c*. (4) Rational actors choose the alternative with the highest ranking. and (5) They take the same decision each time they are confronted with the same set of options.

4. The term 'valence' originates from psychology where it describes a set of emotions (positive or negative) towards a specific object (Frijda 1986: 207).

5. Enelow and Hinich (1982), moreover, claim that on valence issues voters share the same ideal points. On position issues, however, they have different ideal points.

6. Budge and Farlie refer to their theory as *saliency theory*. While the expression "issue ownership" was introduced by John Petrocik (1996: 825), the authors repeatedly use the term "ownership" throughout their work (e.g. 1983: 25, 41, 158).

7. On the stability of issue ownership on the aggregate level, see Bélanger (2003); Brasher (2009); Egan (2013); Green and Jennings (2012a); Lanz and Sciarini (2016); Lutz and Sciarini (2016); and Nadeau et al. (2001).

8. Note that Bélanger (2003), too, analyses issue ownership in Canada. Since the analysis, however, does not link party competence ratings with the vote, I refrain from discussing the findings.

9. For the distinction between position and valence issues, see section 2.2.

10. Van der Brug (2004), moreover, models issue ownership voting based on the logic of directional voting (Rabinowitz and Macdonald 1989). "When valence issues are at stake the preferences of all actors have the same direction. Differences in preferences thus manifest themselves only in the priorities given to issues, i.e. intensities. Scalar products can then be expressed as the products of the intensity of respondents and the intensity of parties" (van der Brug 2004: 217). The empirical test yields mixed results, which lead the author to reject the directional hypothesis.

11. Lutz (2012) observes this in two successive Swiss national elections (2011 and 2015). In both cases, the right-wing Swiss People's Party (SVP) is the owner of the immigration issue in terms of association but not in terms of competence.

12. The number of coefficients is twenty since the impact of five issues is estimated for the five largest parties.

13. A party system is competitive if many actors compete (fragmented system), the parties' ideological positions are distinct (high polarization), and the threshold for winning a seat is low (high proportionality).

14. Note that Lachat uses the term "single-issue voting" (2011: 646). This term was originally introduced by Conover, Gray, and Coombs (1982). However, their definition of single-issue voting is different than Lachat's: "The term typically denotes an issue that stimulates people to behave in a single-minded fashion, in the sense that the issue totally dominates other considerations" (1982: 310). Strictly speaking, this issue does not have to be the most salient nor does single issue voting contain the notion of issue-handling competence.

3. THEORETICAL FRAMEWORK

1. But see the ongoing debate on issue trespassing. Some claim that confronting the adversary party on the same issue might pay off electorally (e.g. Hayes 2005); others find that this is not a good campaign strategy (e.g. Norpoth and Buchanan 1992).

2. Like Green-Pedersen and Mortensen (2015), Meguid (2005) uses the CMP dataset in her analysis.

3. Walgrave and De Swert (2007) and Walgrave, Lefevere, and Nuytemans (2009) look at media data instead of manifestos. They find that media reports play an important role in shaping issue ownership.

4. The authors use the economy as an example for a performance issue.

5. For a detailed description of retrospective voting and its counterpart, prospective voting, see Key (1966).

6. Note that I use the terms 'party identification' and 'partisanship' interchangeably (see e.g. Fiorina 2002).

7. Note that partisanship is measured, rather unconventionally, on a 7-point scale, where 0 means strong identification with left-wing parties and 1 indicates strong identification with right-wing parties.

8. See the discussion on the perceptual screen earlier in this section.

9. Only when the party identification is on its lowest value (i.e. 0 on a 0–10 scale), the positive effect of news on competence is statistically insignificant (Walgrave, Lefevere, and Tresch 2014: 13).

10. In a recent article, Lefevere et al. (2017) investigate positional cues in questions about issue competence. They argue that the wording 'has the best ideas' contains an explicit positional cue. It is only a small leap to arguing that 'agree with the ideas' also contains such cues.

11. Note that this wording is slightly different from the one I use to measure party competence on the MIP: "Which [party/presidential candidate] do you think is best in dealing with it" (see table 4.2).

12. Note that De Sio and Weber (2014) use the term *saliency theory* instead of *issue ownership theory*. Throughout the literature, these terms are often used interchangeably (Budge 2015). However, usually the saliency theory is associated with Budge and Farlie's work, while the issue ownership points to Petrocik's contributions.

13. Note that in the US context, abortion is one of Stokes's prime example of a position issue (1985: 24).

14. See also Krosnick (1988a).

15. For a critical account on the role of issue salience in the decision-making process, see Niemi and Bartels (1985).

16. Lachat (2015) makes the same argument in the case of proximity voting.

17. The terms 'polarization' and 'ideological convergence' are used interchangeably (Green and Hobolt 2008).

18. Proportionality measures the electoral threshold. Proportionality is related to fragmentation, which makes it hard to distinguish their separate effects (Lachat 2011: 653–654).

19. Lachat (2011) uses the term *single-issue voting*. This term was coined by Conover, Gray, and Coombs (1982) where it has a different meaning than in Lachat's analysis: "The term typically denotes an issue that stimulates people to behave in a single-minded fashion, in the sense that the issue totally dominates other considerations" (Conover, Gray, and Coombs 1982: 310).

20. For the zero-sum argument, see also Sanders (1999).

21. Note that the authors use the perceived distance between the Labour Party and the Conservative Party to measure party system polarization (Green and Hobolt 2008: 464). Compared to traditional indicators of polarization, this measure does not factor in the electoral strength of a party (Dalton 2008).

22. Note that rejecting the zero-sum hypothesis is not central to the polarization hypothesis of the second camp. In fact, Pardos-Prado (2012: 343) posits that the

zero-sum hypothesis might be unrelated to the polarization hypothesis. Put differently, the weakening of the proximity model might not be connected to an increase of competence-based voting due to high levels of ideological diversion.

23. Note that I present partial models in the online appendix. A comparison with the full models shows that the effect of voter-party distance and government performance decreases in strength once I control for partisanship. This indicates that the sources are related to each other.

24. See the questionnaire of the third module on the CSES web page: http://www. cses.org.

4. EMPIRICAL FRAMEWORK

1. Translation: Mrs Merkel is plenty incompetent. She depends on her bureaucrats, who tell her what to do and what not to do.

2. Note that I exclude Japan since the survey concerns an Upper House election in which only half of the seats were up for election. I further drop Ireland because the question on the MIP is not available.

3. Each country is not included in at least two of the three data projects. The United States is not included in the ParlGov project. In this case, I gathered the information on my own.

4. UK data are available on http://www.britishelectionstudy.com. Italian data are available on http://www.itanes.org.

5. See the project webpages https://freedomhouse.org and http://www.systemicpeace.org.

6. Alternative data sources are the ESS and the True European Voter Project (TEV). While the 2009 EES dataset contains questions on issue importance and party competence, it is limited to member countries of the EU. Moreover, the data are gathered in the context of the European Parliament elections. The data include a question on the vote choice in the last national election. However, in some countries, this election was four years prior to the interview date which might impose bias to the answers. Due to data availability, the TEV is not suitable either. By the time I conducted the empirical analysis for this project, the data were not yet released. Other studies sometimes used in electoral research do not contain issue ownership items (e.g. the World Value Survey or the Eurobarometer).

7. The dataset is available on the project web page: http://www.cses.org/.

8. The CSES currently consists of four modules (a fifth module is planned) with varying items and participating countries. Unfortunately, the first (1996–2001), second (2001–2006), and fourth (2011–2016) modules do not contain questions on party issue competence.

9. For reasons of simplicity, I will nevertheless refer to the voter data as 'CSES data'.

10. CSES, question Q1b.

11. The CSES asks respondents about the second MIP (Q2b) and the party best able to handle this issue (Q3b). I do not use this question since it has been answered

by only approximately half of the respondents. The number of cases in the analysis would decrease by more than 9,000 voters who only provided an MIP. In my opinion, the advantages of including the second MIP to the analysis does not compensate for dropping these respondents.

12. Wagner and Zeglovits (2014), moreover, consider the use of heuristics as a third measurement error. They argue that competence evaluations might be distorted by partisanship and position. I do not agree with labelling the use of heuristics as a measurement error. In chapter 5, I argue that partisanship and position should be acknowledged as two important sources of individual party competence ratings.

13. To avoid repetition, I also refer to party identification as 'partisanship'.

14. For a similar strategy, see Therriault (2015).

15. Instead of the left-right axis, the conservative-liberal axis is used in the United States.

16. Positions of the following parties are imputed: TOP 09 (Czech Republic), Public affairs (VV, Czech Republic), Freedom and Solidarity (SaS, Slovakia), Most – Hid (MH, Slovakia), and the Social Liberals (Zares, Slovenia).

17. The terms 'political knowledge' and 'political sophistication' are used interchangeably.

18. The full list of questions is provided in the codebook of the CSES: http://www.cses.org/ datacenter/module3/module3.htm.

19. The database is available on the project web page: http://www.parlgov.org/.

20. The database is available on: http://www.cpds-data.org.

21. The CMP database is available on https://manifestoproject.wzb.eu/.

22. The coding scheme is provided in the online appendix.

23. Benoit, Laver, and Mikhaylov (2009: 125) note that "almost all" of the hundreds of published studies use the CMP to estimate positions of parties on the left-right scale.

24. The exact codes are 'multiculturalism positive' (per607), 'multiculturalism negative' (per608), and 'underprivileged minority groups' (per705).

25. Denmark and Switzerland are outliers in this regard. In both countries, one-fifth of the electorate considers immigration the MIP.

26. Some analyses measure polarization on additional dimensions (e.g. Goldberg and Sciarini 2014; Lachat 2011). I focus on the left-right dimension since this is the primary political dimension in all countries. The meaning and the importance of any additional dimension vary across the countries.

27. Note that this includes the entire electorate and not only the supporters of party j.

5. THE SOURCES OF ISSUE OWNERSHIP

1. Nominal variables are a subcategory of categorical variables (Long and Freese 2001: 4).

2. This transpires from the specifications of the systematic components in the utility functions: $V_{ij} = x_{ij}\beta_j$ for MNLM and $V_{ij} = z_{ij}\gamma$ for CLM.

3. Since the post-election studies in Italy and the UK do not contain information on government performance, H2 is not tested in these countries.

4. A discussion on how the observed-outcome approach compares to estimating the predicted probabilities for fixed outcomes (in the context of the full issue ownership voting model) is provided in the online appendix.

5. These values are prominently featured in King, Tomz, and Wittenberg (2000). Due to the Bayesian framework, I proceed slightly different than King, Tomz, and Wittenberg. Instead of sampling from the parameters, I use the MCMC-generated samples.

6. In addition to the full models, I run models containing one source of competence ratings at a time (online appendix). A comparison of the full models with the partial models shows how much the effect of one source decreases once I control for alternative sources of issue ownership. While the FDs generally decrease, only little changes occur in terms of the effect signs.

7. The online appendix is available on https://simonlanz.com

8. Gariup (2013: 17) argues that Switzerland has the all the features of a low-clarity case.

9. 'Incumbency' status is constant across voters x_j.

10. Theoretically, 11 is the maximum value of the distance variable. However, this is possible only if the party occupies an extreme position in the political spectrum (position party $\in \{0,10\}$) and the voter has the other extreme position. In practice, this is never the case. For instance, the Spanish party PSOE has a position of 3.7 (moderate left). Hence, the maximal distance score is 6.3.

6. ISSUE OWNERSHIP VOTING

1. For more information on the hybrid model, see section 5.1.

2. The reference category is the economy. The following abbreviations are used in the equations: social (social policy), external (external relations), services (public services), and quality (quality of live).

3. I, moreover, estimate the predicted probabilities and FDs for the smallest and the largest parties in the country. In the full model, FDs are slightly higher when I predict the vote for the largest party (0.16 for large parties; 0.12 for small parties). A more detailed discussion of the observed-outcome approach is provided in the online appendix.

4. Note that I estimate models where competence evaluation is the only input variable $V_{ij} = \beta_{0j} + \gamma_1 \text{ competent}_{ij}$ (online appendix). A comparison of these crude models with the baseline models (equation 6.1) gives us an idea about how much the effect of competence changes if I control for gender, age, education, political sophistication, and the MIP. As it turns out, this decrease is minimal. The average FD decreases from 0.46 (models without controls) to 0.42 (baseline models).

5. Note that this model excludes Slovenia, Italy, and the UK due to missing variables (i.e. political sophistication and performance).

7. ISSUE OWNERSHIP VOTING ACROSS CONTEXTS

1. As will transpire from the next section, it is actually a three-dimensional array, where the third dimension is the countries.

2. I also ran a single model with an interaction term between party competence ratings and polarization/fragmentation/clarity. Unfortunately, the chains of the contextual regressors and the interactions did not converge to the stationary. I, thus, refrain from presenting these results.

3. A linear regression analysis shows that the positive slope is highly credible (analysis not shown). Further, the effect holds in a feasible generalized least squares regression (Lewis and Linzer 2005: 351). In addition to a standard linear regression, this model takes into account the uncertainty (HPDs) associated with the observations on the outcome.

4. The direction of the OLS slope changes from slightly negative to slightly positive if I exclude the United States and Spain (not shown). In general, the effect remains weak and uncertain.

References

Aalberg, Toril and Anders Todal Jenssen. 2007. 'Do Television Debates in Multiparty Systems Affect Viewers? A Quasi-Experimental Study with First-time Voters'. *Scandinavian Political Studies* 30(1):115–135.

Adams, James. 2001. *Party Competition and Responsible Party Government*. Ann Arbor: University of Michigan Press.

Adams, James, Samuel Merrill, and Bernard Grofman. 2005. *A Unified Theory of Party Competition: A Cross-National Analysis Integrating Spatial and Behavioral Factors*. Cambridge: Cambridge University Press.

Akkerman, Tjitske, Sarah L. de Lange, and Matthijs Rooduijn. 2016. 'Into the Mainstream? A Comparative Analysis of the Programmatic Profiles of Radical Right-Wing Populist Parties in Western Europe over Time'. In *Radical Right-Wing Populist Parties in Western Europe: Into the Mainstream?* ed. Matthijs Rooduijn, Tjitske Akkerman, and Sarah L. de Lange. London: Routledge, pp. 31–53.

Aldrich, John H. and Richard D. McKelvey. 1977. 'A Method of Scaling with Applications to the 1968 and 1972 Presidential Elections'. *American Political Science Review* 71(1):111–130.

Alt, James E. 1979. *The Politics of Economic Decline: Economic Management and Political Behaviour in Britain since 1964*. Cambridge: Cambridge University Press.

Alvarez, R. Michael. 1997. *Information and Elections*. Ann Arbor: The University of Michigan Press.

Alvarez, R. Michael and Jonathan Nagler. 1995. 'Economics, Issues and the Perot Candidacy: Voter Choice in the 1992 Presidential Election'. *American Journal of Political Science* 39(3):714–744.

Alvarez, R. Michael and Jonathan Nagler. 1998. 'When Politics and Models Collide: Estimating Models of Multiparty Elections'. *American Journal of Political Science* 42(1):55–96.

Alvarez, R. Michael and Jonathan Nagler. 2004. 'Party System Compactness: Measurement and Consequences'. *Political Analysis* 12(1):46–62.

Anand, Sowmya and J. A. Krosnick. 2003. 'The Impact of Attitudes toward Foreign Policy Goals on Public Preferences among Presidential Candidates: A Study of Issue Publics and the Attentive Public in the 2000 U.S. Presidential Election'. *Presidential Studies Quarterly* 33(1):31–71.

Anderson, Cameron D. 2006. 'Economic Voting and Multilevel Governance: A Comparative Individual-Level Analysis'. *American Journal of Political Science* 50(2):449–463.

Anderson, Christopher J. 2000. 'Economic Voting and Political Context: A Comparative Perspective'. *Electoral Studies* 19(2–3):151–170.

Anderson, Christopher J. 2007. 'The Interaction of Structures and Voter Behavior'. In *Oxford Handbook of Political Behavior*, ed. Russel J. Dalton and Hans-Dieter Klingemann. Oxford: Oxford University Press, pp. 589–609.

Armingeon, Klaus, Virginia Wenger, Fiona Wiedemeier, Christian Isler, Laura Knöpfel, David Weisstanner, and Sarah Engler. 2017. *Comparative Political Data Set 1960–2015*. Bern: Institute of Political Science, University of Bern.

Arrow, Kenneth J. 1951. *Social Choice and Individual Values*. New York: Wiley.

Ashworth, Scott and Ethan Bueno De Mesquita. 2014. 'Is Voter Competence Good for Voters? Information, Rationality, and Democratic Performance'. *American Political Science Review* 108(3):565–587.

Baker, Kendall L., Russell J. Dalton, and Kai Hildebrandt. 1981. *Germany Transformed: Political Culture and the New Politics*. Cambridge, MA: Harvard University Press.

Bakker, Ryan, Catherine de Vries, Erica Edwards, Liesbet Hooghe, Seth Jolly, Gary Marks, Jonathan Polk, Jan Rovny, Marco Steenbergen and Milada Anna Vachudova. 2015. 'Measuring Party Positions in Europe: The Chapel Hill Expert Survey Trend File, 1999–2010'. *Party Politics* 21(1):143–152.

Bartels, Larry M. 1996. 'Uninformed Votes: Information Effects in Presidential Elections'. *American Journal of Political Science* 40(1):194–230.

Bartels, Larry M. 2002. 'Beyond the Running Tally: Partisan Bias in Political Perceptions'. *Political Behavior* 24(2):117–150.

Bartels, Larry M. 2010. 'The Study of Electoral Behavior'. In *The Oxford Handbook of American Elections and Political Behavior*, ed. Jan E. Leighley. Oxford: Oxford University Press, pp. 239–262.

Bartolini, Stefano and Peter Mair. 1990. *Identity, Competition, and Electoral Availability: The Stabilisation of European Electorates 1885–1985*. Cambridge: Cambridge University Press.

Bélanger, Eric. 2003. 'Issue Ownership by Canadian Political Parties 1953–2001'. *Canadian Journal of Political Science* 36(3):539–558.

Bélanger, Eric and Bonnie M. Meguid. 2008. 'Issue Salience, Issue Ownership, and Issue-Based Vote Choice'. *Electoral Studies* 27(3):477–491.

Bellucci, P. and M. Bull. 2002. 'Introduction. The Return of Berlusconi'. In *The Return of Berlusconi*, ed. P. Bellucci and M. Bull. New York: Berghahn Books, pp. 29–49.

Bellucci, Paolo. 2006. 'Tracing the Cognitive and Affective Roots of Party Competence: Italy and Britain, 2001'. *Electoral Studies* 25(3):548–569.

Benoit, Kenneth and Michael Laver. 2006. *Party Policy in Modern Democracies*. London: Routledge.

Benoit, Kenneth, Michael Laver, and Slava Mikhaylov. 2009. 'Treating Words as Data with Error: Uncertainty in Text Statements of Policy Positions'. *American Journal of Political Science* 53(2):495–513.

Benoit, William L. and Glenn J. Hansen. 2004. 'Issue Ownership in Primary and General Presidential Debates'. *Argumentation and Advocacy* 40(3):143–154.

Berelson, Bernard, Paul Lazarsfeld, and William McPhee. 1954. *Voting: A Study of Opinion Formation in a Presidential Campaign*. Chicago: University of Chicago Press.

Borre, Ole. 2001. *Issue Voting: An Introduction*. Arhus: Aarhus University Press.

Brambor, Thomas, William Roberts Clark, and Matt Golder. 2006. 'Understanding Interaction Models: Improving Empirical Analyses'. *Political Analysis* 14(1):63–82.

Brasher, Holly. 2009. 'The Dynamic Character of Political Party Evaluations'. *Party Politics* 15(1):69–92.

Brody, Richard A. and Benjamin I. Page. 1972. 'Comment: The Assessment of Policy Voting'. *American Political Science Review* 66(2):450–458.

Budge, Ian. 2000. 'Expert Judgements of Party Policy Positions: Uses and Limitations in Political Research'. *European Journal of Political Research* 37(1):103–113.

Budge, Ian. 2015. 'Issue Emphases, Saliency Theory and Issue Ownership: A Historical and Conceptual Analysis'. *West European Politics* 38(4):761–777.

Budge, Ian and Dennis Farlie. 1983. *Explaining and Predicting Elections: Issue Effects and Party Strategies in Twenty-Three Democracies*. London: Allen and Unwin.

Budge, Ian, David Robertson, and Derek Hearl. 1987. *Ideology, Strategy and Party Change*. Cambridge: Cambridge University Press.

Campbell, Angus, Philip E. Converse, Warren E. Miller, and Donald E. Stokes. 1960. *The American Voter*. New York: Wiley.

Campbell, James E., Mary Munro, John R. Alford, and Bruce R. Campbell. 1986. 'Partisanship and Voting'. In *Research in Micropolitics*, ed. Samuel Long. Greenwich, CT: JAI Press, pp. 99–126.

Carpini, Michael X. Delli and Scott Keeter. 1991. 'Stability and Change in the U.S. Public's Knowledge of Politics'. *The Public Opinion Quarterly* 55(4):583–612.

Carsey, Thomas M. and Geoffrey C. Layman. 2006. 'Changing Sides or Changing Minds? Party Identification and Policy Preferences in the American Electorate'. *American Journal of Political Science* 50(2):464–477.

Castels, Francis G. and Peter Mair. 1984. 'Left-Right Political Scales: Some Expert Judgments'. *European Journal of Political Research* 12(1):73–88.

Chaiken, Shelly. 1980. 'Heuristic Versus Systematic Information Processing and the Use of Source versus Message Cues in Persuasion'. *Journal of Personality and Social Psychology* 39(5):752–766.

Christensen, Love, Stefan Dahlberg, and Johan Martinsson. 2015. 'Changes and Fluctuations in Issue Ownership: The Case of Sweden'. *Scandinavian Political Studies* 38(2):137–157.

Claassen, Ryan L. 2009. 'Direction versus Proximity'. *American Politics Research* 37(2):227–253.

Clarke, H., D. Sanders, M. Stewart, and P. Whiteley. 2004. *Political Choice in Britain*. Oxford: Oxford University Press.

Conover, Pamela Johnston, Virginia Gray, and Steven Coombs. 1982. 'Single-Issue Voting: Elite-Mass Linkages'. *Political Behavior* 4(4):309–331.

Converse, Philip E. 1969. 'Of Time and Partisan Stability'. *Comparative Political Studies* 2(2):139–171.

Converse, Philip E. and Roy Pierce. 1985. 'Measuring Partisanship'. *Political Methodology* 11(3–4):143–166.

Coombs, Clyde H. 1950. 'Psychological Scaling without a Unit of Measurement'. *Psychological Review* 57(3):145–158.

Crewe, Ivor and David Denver. 1985. *Electoral Change in Western Democracies: Patterns and Sources of Electoral Volatility*. New York: Palgrave Macmillan.

Curtice, John. 2002. 'The State of Election Studies: Mid-Life Crisis or New Youth?' *Electoral Studies* 21(2):161–168.

Dahlberg, Stefan and Johan Martinsson. 2015. 'Changing Issue Ownership through Policy Communication'. *West European Politics* 38(4):817–838.

Dalton, Russell J. 1984. 'Cognitive Mobilization and Partisan Dealignment in Advanced Industrial Democracies'. *The Journal of Politics* 46(1):264–284.

Dalton, Russel J. 1996. *Citizen Politics: Public Opinion and Political Parties in Advanced Industrial Democracies*. Chatham: Chatham House.

Dalton, Russell J. 2008. 'The Quantity and the Quality of Party Systems: Party System Polarization, Its Measurement, and Its Consequences'. *Comparative Political Studies* 41(7):899–920.

Dalton, Russel J. and Christopher J. Anderson. 2010. 'Citizens, Context, and Choice'. In *Citizens, Context, and Choice: How Context Shapes Citizens' Electoral Choices*, ed. Russel J. Dalton and Christopher J. Anderson. Oxford: Oxford University Press, pp. 3–33.

Dalton, Russel J., Scott E. Flanagan, and Paul A. Beck. 1984. *Electoral Change in Advanced Industrial Democracies: Realignment or Dealignment?* Princeton, NJ: Princeton University Press.

Damore, David F. 2004. 'The Dynamics of Issue Ownership in Presidential Campaigns'. *Political Research Quarterly* 57(3):391–397.

De Bruycker, Iskander and Stefaan Walgrave. 2014. 'How a New Issue Becomes an Owned Issue. Media Coverage and the Financial Crisis in Belgium'. *International Journal of Public Opinion Research* 26(1):86–97.

De Sio, Lorenzo and Till Weber. 2014. 'Issue Yield: A Model of Party Strategy in Multidimensional Space'. *American Political Science Review* 108(4):870–885.

de Vries, Catherine E., Erica E. Edwards, and Erik R. Tillman. 2011. 'Clarity of Responsibility Beyond the Pocketbook: How Political Institutions Condition EU Issue Voting'. *Comparative Political Studies* 44(3):339–363.

Döring, Holger and Philip Manow. 2016. *Parliaments and Governments Database (ParlGov): Information on Parties, Elections and Cabinets in Modern Democracies*. Bremen: University of Bremen.

Dorussen, Han and Michaell Taylor. 2001. 'The Political Context of Issue-Priority Voting: Coalitions and Economic Voting in the Netherlands, 1970–1999'. *Electoral Studies* 20(3):399–426.

Downs, Anthony. 1957. *An Economic Theory of Democracy*. New York: Harper.

Druckman, James N., Erik Peterson, and Rune Slothuus. 2013. 'How Elite Partisan Polarization Affects Public Opinion Formation'. *American Political Science Review* 107(1):57–79.

Eagly, Alice H. and Shelly Chaiken. 1993. *The Psychology of Attitudes*. Fort Worth, TX: Harcourt Brace Jovanovich.

Egan, Patrick J. 2013. *Partisan Priorities. How Issue Ownership Drives and Distorts American Politics*. Cambridge: Cambridge University Press.

Eichhorn, Wolfgang. 2005. *Agenda-Setting-Prozesse. Eine theoretische Analyse individueller und gesellschaftlicher Themenstrukturierung*. München: Reinhard Fischer.

Enelow, James M. and Melvin J. Hinich. 1982. 'Nonspatial Candidate Characteristics and Electoral Competition'. *The Journal of Politics* 44(1):115–130.

Enelow, James M. and Melvin J. Hinich. 1984. *The Spatial Theory of Voting: An Introduction*. Cambridge: Cambridge University Press.

Erikson, Robert S. and David W. Romero. 1990. 'Candidate Equilibrium and the Behavioral Model of the Vote'. *American Political Science Review* 84(4):1103–1126.

Evans, Geoffrey. 1999. 'Economics and Politics Revisited: Exploring the Decline in Conservative Support, 1992–1995'. *Political Studies* 47(1):139–151.

Fiorina, Morris. 1981. *Retrospective Voting in American National Elections*. New Haven, CT: Yale University Press.

Fiorina, Morris. 2002. 'Parties and Partisanship: A 40-Year Retrospective'. *Political Behavior* 24(2):93–115.

Forgas, Joseph P. 2008. 'Affect and Cognition'. *Perspectives on Psychological Science* 3(2):94–101.

Fournier, Patrick, André Blais, Richard Nadeau, Elisabeth Gidengil and Neil Nevitte. 2003. 'Issue Importance and Performance Voting'. *Political Behavior* 25(1):51–67.

Franklin, Mark. 1985. 'Assessing the Rise of Issue Voting in British Elections since 1964'. *Electoral Studies* 4(1):37–56.

Franklin, Mark. 1992. 'The Decline of Cleavage Politics'. In *Electoral Change*, ed. Mark Franklin, Thomas Mackie, and Henry Valem. Cambridge: Cambridge University Press, pp. 383–405.

Franklin, Mark and Christopher Wlezien. 2002. 'Reinventing Election Studies'. *Electoral Studies* 21(2):331–338.

Friedrich, Robert J. 1982. 'In Defense of Multiplicative Terms in Multiple Regression Equations'. *American Journal of Political Science* 26(4):797–833.

Frijda, Nico H. 1986. *The Emotions*. Cambridge: Cambridge University Press.

Gabel, Matthew J. and John D. Huber. 2000. 'Putting Parties in Their Place: Inferring Party Left-Right Ideological Positions from Party Manifestos Data'. *American Journal of Political Science* 44(1):94–103.

Gariup, Deana. 2013. 'The Economy Matters. Exploring Economic Voting in Swiss Federal Elections'. Geneva Laboratory of Political Science, Department of Political Science and International Relations, University of Geneva.

Gelman, Andrew and Jennifer Hill. 2007. *Data Analysis Using Regression and Multilevel/Hierarchical Models*. Cambridge: Cambridge University Press.

Giger, Nathalie. 2011. *The Risk of Social Policy? The Electoral Consequences of Welfare State Retrenchment and Social Policy Performance in OECD Countries*. London: Routledge.

Giger, Nathalie and Simon Hug. 2018. 'An Error Grave of Consequence. Empirical Models to Study Propensities to Vote for Parties'. *Working Paper*.

Goldberg, Andreas C. and Pascal Sciarini. 2014. 'Electoral Competition and the New Class Cleavage'. *Swiss Political Science Review* 20(4):573–589.

Goldberg, Andreas C. and Simon Lanz. 2019. 'Living abroad, voting as if at home? Electoral motivations of expatriates'. *Migration Studies.*

Goren, Paul. 2002. 'Character Weakness, Partisan Bias, and Presidential Evaluation'. *American Journal of Political Science* 46(3):627–641.

Goren, Paul. 2005. 'Party Identification and Core Political Values'. *American Journal of Political Science* 49(4):881–896.

Green, Jane. 2007. 'When Voters and Parties Agree: Valence Issues and Party Competition'. *Political Studies* 55(3):629–655.

Green, Jane and Sara B. Hobolt. 2008. 'Owning the Issue Agenda: Party Strategies and Vote Choices in British Elections'. *Electoral Studies* 27(3):460–476.

Green, Jane and Will Jennings. 2012a. 'The Dynamics of Issue Competence and Vote for Parties in and out of Power: An Analysis of Valence in Britain, 1979–1997'. *European Journal of Political Research* 51(4):469–503.

Green, Jane and Will Jennings. 2012b. 'Valence as Macro-Competence: An Analysis of Mood in Party Competence Evaluations in Great Britain'. *British Journal of Political Science* 42(2):311–343.

Green-Pedersen, Christoffer. 2007. 'The Growing Importance of Issue Competition: The Changing Nature of Party Competition in Western Europe'. *Political Studies* 55(3):607–628.

Green-Pedersen, Christoffer and Peter B. Mortensen. 2015. 'Avoidance and Engagement: Issue Competition in Multiparty Systems'. *Political Studies* 63(4):747–764.

Hanmer, Michael J. and Kerem Ozan Kalkan. 2013. 'Behind the Curve: Clarifying the Best Approach to Calculating Predicted Probabilities and Marginal Effects from Limited Dependent Variable Models'. *American Journal of Political Science* 57(1):263–277.

Hayes, Danny. 2005. 'Candidate Qualities through a Partisan Lens: A Theory of Trait Ownership'. *American Journal of Political Science* 49(4):908–923.

Hobolt, Sara, James Tilley, and Susan Banducci. 2013. 'Clarity of Responsibility: How Government Cohesion Conditions Performance Voting'. *European Journal of Political Research* 52(2):164–187.

Holbrook, Allyson L., Matthew K. Berent, Jon A. Krosnick, Penny S. Visser, and David S. Boninger. 2005. 'Attitude Importance and the Accumulation of Attitude-Relevant Knowledge in Memory'. *Journal of Personality and Social Psychology* 88(5):749–769.

Holian, David B. 2004. 'He's Stealing My Issues! Clinton's Crime Rhetoric and the Dynamics of Issue Ownership'. *Political Behavior* 26(2):95–124.

Hotelling, Harold. 1929. 'Stability in Competition'. *The Economic Journal* 39(153):41–57.

Howard Schuman, Jacob Ludwig, and Jon A. Krosnick. 1986. 'The Perceived Threat of Nuclear War, Salience, and Open Questions'. *The Public Opinion Quarterly* 50(4):519–536.

Huber, John and Ronald Inglehart. 1995. 'Expert Interpretations of Party Space and Party Locations in 42 Societies'. *Party Politics* 1(1):73–111.

Hyman, Herbert. 1959. *Political Socialization*. Glencoe: The Free Press.

Irwin, Galen A. and Joseph J. M. van Holsteyn. 1989. 'Towards a More Open Model of Competition'. *West European Politics* 12(1):112–138.

Iyengar, S. and D. R. Kinder. 1987. *News that Matters: Television and American Opinion*. Chicago: The University of Chicago Press.

Iyengar, Shanto. 1990. 'Framing Responsibility for Political Issues: The Case of Poverty'. *Political Behavior* 12(1):19–40.

Jackman, Simon. 2009. *Bayesian Analysis for the Social Sciences*. New York: Wiley.

Jackson, John E. 1975. 'Issues, Party Choices, and Presidential Votes'. *American Journal of Political Science* 19(2):161–185.

Jennings, M. Kent. 2007. 'Political Socialization'. In *The Oxford Handbook of Political Behavior*, ed. Russel J. Dalton and Hans-Dieter Klingemann. Oxford: Oxford University Press, pp. 29–45.

Jennings, M. Kent and Richard G. Niemi. 1981. *Generations and Politics: A Panel Study of Young Adults and Their Parents*. Princeton, NJ: Princeton University Press.

Jennings, Will and Christopher Wlezien. 2011. 'Distinguishing between Most Important Problems and Issues?' *The Public Opinion Quarterly* 75(3):545–555.

Johnson, M., W. Phillips Shively, and R. M. Stein. 2002. 'Contextual Data and the Study of Elections and Voting Behavior: Connecting Individuals to Environments'. *Electoral Studies* 21(2):219–233.

Jones, Bryan D. 1994. *Reconceiving Decision-Making in Democratic Politics: Attention, Choice, and Public Policy*. Chicago: University of Chicago Press.

Kam, Cindy D. and Robert J. Franzese. 2007. *Modeling and Interpreting Interactive Hypotheses in Regression Analysis*. Ann Arbor: University of Michigan Press.

Key, V. O. 1966. *The Responsible Electorate. Rationality in Presidential Voting. 1936–1960*. New York: The Belknap Press of Harvard University Press.

Kinder, Donald R. and D. O. Sears. 1985. 'Public Opinion and Political Action'. In *Handbook of Social Psychology*, ed. G. Lindzey and E. Aronson. New York: Random House, pp. 659–741.

King, Gary, Michael Tomz, and Jason Wittenberg. 2000. 'Making the Most of Statistical Analyses: Improving Interpretation and Presentation'. *American Journal of Political Science* 44(2):347–361.

Kittilson, Miki Caul and Christopher J. Anderson. 2011. 'Electoral Supply and Voter Turnout'. In *Citizens, Context, and Choice*, ed. Russel J. Dalton and Christopher J. Anderson. Oxford: Oxford University Press, pp. 33–55.

Kleinnijenhuis, Jan and Annemarie S. Walter. 2014. 'News, Discussion, and Associative Issue Ownership: Instability at the Micro Level versus Stability at the Macro Level'. *The International Journal of Press/Politics* 19(2):226–245.

Klingemann, Hans-Dieter, Richard Hofferbert, and Ian Budge. 1994. *Parties, Policies, and Democracy*. Boulder, CO: Westview Press.

Klingemann, Hans-Dieter, Andrea Volkens, Judith Bara, Ian Budge, and Michael D. McDonald. 2006. *Mapping Policy Preferences II: Estimates for Parties, Electors, and Governments in Eastern Europe, European Union, and OECD 1990–2003*. Oxford: Oxford University Press.

Klüver, Heike and Jae-Jae Spoon. 2016. 'Who Responds? Voters, Parties and Issue Attention'. *British Journal of Political Science* 46(3):633–654.

Kramer, Gerald H. 1971. 'Short-Term Fluctuations in U.S. Voting Behavior, 1896–1964'. *American Political Science Review* 65(1):131–143.

Kriesi, Hanspeter, Edgar Grande, Romain Lachat, Martin Dolezal, Simon Bornschier, and Timotheos Frey. 2008. *West European Politics in the Age of Globalization*. Cambridge: Cambridge University Press.

Kroh, Martin. 2003. *Parties, Politicians, and Policies*. Amsterdam: Amsterdam School of Communication Research.

Kroh, Martin. 2009. 'The Ease of Ideological Voting: Voter Sophistication and Party System Complexity'. In *The Comparative Study of Electoral Systems*, ed. Hans-Dieter Klingemann. Oxford: Oxford University Press, pp. 220–236.

Krosnick, Jon A. 1988a. 'Attitude Importance and Attitude Change'. *Journal of Experimental Social Psychology* 24(3):240–255.

Krosnick, Jon A. 1988b. 'The Role of Attitude Importance in Social Evaluation: A Study of Policy Preferences, Presidential Candidate Evaluations, and Voting Behavior'. *Journal of Personality and Social Psychology* 55(2):196–210.

Krosnick, Jon A. and Donald R. Kinder. 1990. 'Altering the Foundations of Support for the President through Priming'. *American Political Science Review* 84(2):497–512.

Krosnick, Jon A. and Laura A. Brannon. 1993. 'The Impact of the Gulf War on the Ingredients of Presidential Evaluations: Multidimensional Effects of Political Involvement'. *American Political Science Review* 87(4):963–975.

Krosnick, Jon A., Penny S. Visser, and Joshua Harder. 2010. 'The Psychological Underpinnings of Political Behavior'. In *Handbook of Social Psychology*, ed. Susan T. Fiske, Daniel T. Gilbert, and Lindzey Gardner. New York: Wiley, pp. 1288–1342.

Kruschke, John. 2014. *Doing Bayesian Data Analysis, Second Edition: A Tutorial with R, JAGS, and Stan*. London: Academic Press.

Kuechler, Manfred. 1991. 'Issues and Voting in the European Elections 1989'. *European Journal of Political Research* 19(1):81–103.

Laakso, Markku and Rein Taagepera. 1979. 'Effective Number of Parties: A Measure with Application to West Europe'. *Comparative Political Studies* 12(1):3–27.

Lachat, Romain. 2011. 'Electoral Competitiveness and Issue Voting'. *Political Behavior* 33(4):645–663.

Lachat, Romain. 2014. 'Issue Ownership and the Vote: The Effects of Associative and Competence Ownership on Issue Voting'. *Swiss Political Science Review* 20(4):727–740.

Lachat, Romain. 2015. 'The Role of Party Identification in Spatial Models of Voting Choice'. *Political Science Research and Methods* 3(3):641–658.

Lacy, Dean and Philip Paolino. 1998. 'Downsian Voting and the Separation of Powers'. *American Journal of Political Science* 42(4):1180–1199.

Lanz, Simon. 2012. 'The Importance of Salience. Agenda-Setting and Issue Voting in Swiss Politics'. Geneva Laboratory of Political Science, Department of Political Science and International Relations, University of Geneva.

Lanz, Simon and Pascal Sciarini. 2016. 'The Short-time Dynamics of Issue Ownership and Its Impact on the Vote'. *Journal of Elections, Public Opinion and Parties* 26(2):212–231.

Lau, Richard R. and David P. Redlawsk. 2001. 'Advantages and Disadvantages of Cognitive Heuristics in Political Decision Making'. *American Journal of Political Science* 45(4):951–971.

Lau, Richard R. and David P. Redlawsk. 2006. *How Voters Decide: Information Processing during Election Campaigns*. Cambridge: Cambridge University Press.

Laver, Michael and Ian Budge. 1992. *Party, Policy, and Government Coalitions*. London: St. Martin's Press.

Laver, Michael and John Garry. 2000. 'Estimating Policy Positions from Political Texts'. *American Journal of Political Science* 44(3):619–634.

Lavine, Howard, Christopher Johnston, and Marco Steenbergen. 2012. *The Ambivalent Partisan*. Oxford: Oxford University Press.

Lazarsfeld, Paul F., Bernard Berelson, and Hazel Gaudet. 1944. *The People's Choice. How the Voter Makes Up His Mind in a Presidential Campaign*. New York: Duell, Sloan and Pearce.

Lefevere, Jonas, Rune Stubager, Stefaan Walgrave, and Anke Tresch. 2017. 'Measuring Issue Ownership. A Comparative Question Wording Experiment'. *Scandinavian Political Studies* 40(1):120–131.

Lewis-Beck, Michael S. 1988. *Economics and Elections: The Major Western Democracies*. Ann Arbor: University of Michigan Press.

Lewis-Beck, Michael S., and Mary Stegmaier. 2007. 'Economic Models of Voting'. In *Oxford Handbook of Political Behavior*, ed. Russel J. Dalton and Hans-Dieter Klingemann. Oxford: Oxford University Press, pp. 530–531.

Lewis, Jeffrey B. and Drew A. Linzer. 2005. 'Estimating Regression Models in Which the Dependent Variable Is Based on Estimates'. *Political Analysis* 13(4):345–364.

Lewis, Jeffrey B. and Gary King. 1999. 'No Evidence on Directional vs. Proximity Voting'. *Political Analysis* 8(1):21–33.

Lipset, Seymour M. and Stein Rokkan. 1967. *Cleavage Structures, Party Systems and Voter Alignments: An Introduction*. New York: The Free Press.

Lodge, Milton and Charles S Taber. 2013. *The Rationalizing Voter*. Cambridge: Cambridge University Press.

Long, J. Scott. 1997. *Regression Models for Categorical and Limited Dependent Variables. Advanced Quantitative Techniques in the Social Sciences*. Thousand Oaks, CA: Sage.

Long, J. Scott and Jeremy Freese. 2001. *Regression Models for Categorical Dependent Variables Using Stata*. College Station, TX: Stata Press.

Lowe, Will, Kenneth Benoit, Slava Mikhaylov, and Michael Laver. 2011. 'Scaling Policy Preferences from Coded Political Texts'. *Legislative Studies Quarterly* 36(1):123–155.

Luechinger, Simon, Myra Rosinger, and Alois Stutzer. 2007. 'The Impact of Postal Voting on Participation: Evidence for Switzerland'. *Swiss Political Science Review* 13(2):167–202.

Lutz, Georg. 2012. *Eidgenössische Wahlen 2011. Wahlteilnahme und Wahlentscheid*. Lausanne Selects – FORS.

Lutz, Georg and Pascal Sciarini. 2016. 'Issue Competence and Its Influence on Voting Behavior in the Swiss 2015 Elections'. *Swiss Political Science Review* 22(1):5–14.

Macdonald, Stuart Elaine, George Rabinowitz, and Ola Listhaug. 1997. 'Individual Perception and Models of Issue Voting'. *Journal of Theoretical Politics* 9(1):13–21.

Macdonald, Stuart Elaine, George Rabinowitz, and Ola Listhaug. 1998. 'On Attempting to Rehabilitate the Proximity Model: Sometimes the Patient Just Can't Be Helped'. *The Journal of Politics* 60(3):653–690.

Macdonald, Stuart Elaine, Ola Listhaug, and George Rabinowitz. 1991. 'Issues and Party Support in Multiparty Systems'. *American Political Science Review* 85(4):1107–1131.

Maddens, Bart. 1996. 'Directional Theory of Issue Voting: The Case of the 1991 Parliamentary Elections in Flanders'. *Electoral Studies* 15(1):53–70.

Marsh, Michael. 2002. 'Electoral Context'. *Electoral Studies* 21(2):207–217.

Martinsson, Johan. 2009. *Economic Voting and Issue Ownership. An Integrative Approach.* Gothenburg: Department of Political Science, University of Gothenburg.

Maxwell McCombs, Jian-Hua Zhu. 1995. 'Capacity, Diversity, and Volatility of the Public Agenda: Trends from 1954 to 1994'. *The Public Opinion Quarterly* 59(4):495–525.

McCombs, Maxwell E. and Donald L. Shaw. 1972. 'The Agenda-Setting Function of the Mass Media'. *The Public Opinion Quarterly* 36(2):176–187.

McFadden, Daniel. 1974. 'Conditional Logit Analysis of Qualitative Choice Behavior'. In *Frontiers in Econometrics*, ed. Paul Zarembka. New York: Academic Press, pp. 105–142.

Meguid, Bonnie M. 2005. 'Competition between Unequals: The Role of Mainstream Party Strategy in Niche Party Success'. *American Political Science Review* 99(3):347–359.

Miller, Warren E. and Merril J. Shanks. 1996. *The New American Voter.* Cambridge, MA: Harvard University Press.

Mondak, Jeffery J. 1995. 'Competence, Integrity, and the Electoral Success of Congressional Incumbents'. *The Journal of Politics* 57(4):1043–1069.

Mueller, John. 1973. *War, Presidents, and Public Opinion.* New York: Wiley.

Nadeau, Richard, André Blais, Elisabeth Gidengil, and Neil Nevitte. 2001. 'Perceptions of Party Competence in the 1997 Election'. In *Party Politics in Canada*, ed. Hugh G. Thorburn and Alan Whitehorn. Toronto: Prentice-Hall, pp. 413–430.

Nadeau, Richard, Richard G Niemi, and Antoine Yoshinaka. 2002. 'A Cross-national Analysis of Economic Voting: Taking Account of the Political Context across Time and Nations'. *Electoral Studies* 21(3):403–423.

Neustadt, Richard. 1960. *Presidential Power.* New York: Wiley.

Niemi, Richard G. and Larry M. Bartels. 1985. 'New Measures of Issue Salience: An Evaluation'. *The Journal of Politics* 47(4):1212–1220.

Norpoth, Helmut and Bruce Buchanan. 1992. 'Wanted: The Education President. Issue Trespassing by Political Candidates'. *The Public Opinion Quarterly* 56(1):87–99.

Petitpas, Adrien and Pascal Sciarini. 2018. 'Short-Term Dynamics in Issue Ownership and Electoral Choice Formation'. *Swiss Political Science Review* 24(4):423–441.

Page, Benjamin I. and Calvin C. Jones. 1979. 'Reciprocal Effects of Policy Preferences, Party Loyalties and the Vote'. *American Political Science Review* 73(4):1071–1089.

Page, Benjamin I. and Richard A. Brody. 1972. 'Policy Voting and the Electoral Process: The Vietnam War Issue'. *American Political Science Review* 66(3):979–995.

Page, Benjamin I. and Robert Y. Shapiro. 1992. *The Rational Public: Fifty Years of Trends in Americans' Policy Preferences*. Chicago: University of Chicago Press.

Paldam, Martin. 1991. 'How Robust Is the Vote Function? A Study of Seventeen Countries over Four Decades'. In *Economics and Politics: The Calculus of Support*, ed. Helmut Norpoth, Michael S. Lewis-Beck, and Jean-Dominique Lafay. Ann Arbor: University of Michigan Press, pp. 9–31.

Pardos-Prado, Sergi. 2012. 'Valence beyond Consensus: Party Competence and Policy Dispersion from a Comparative Perspective'. *Electoral Studies* 31(2):342–352.

Petrocik, John R. 1996. 'Issue Ownership in Presidential Elections, with a 1980 Case Study'. *American Journal of Political Science* 40(3):825–850.

Petrocik, John R., William L. Benoit, and Glenn J. Hansen. 2003. 'Issue Ownership and Presidential Campaigning, 1952–2000'. *Political Science Quarterly* 118(4):599–626.

Plummer, Martyn. 2016. *Package rjags*.

Polk, Jonathan, Jan Rovny, Ryan Bakker, Erica Edwards, Liesbet Hooghe, Seth Jolly, Jelle Koedam, Filip Kostelka, Gary Marks, Gijs Schumacher, Marco Steenbergen, Milada Vachudova, and Marko Zilovic. 2017. 'Explaining the Salience of Anti-Elitism and Reducing Political Corruption for Political Parties in Europe with the 2014 Chapel Hill Expert Survey Data'. *Research & Politics* 4(1):1–9.

Powell, G. Bingham. 2000. *Elections as Instruments of Democracy. Majoritarian and Proportional Visions*. New Haven, CT: Yale University Press.

Powell, G. Bingham. 2004. 'Political Representation in Comparative Politics'. *Annual Review of Political Science* 7(1):273–296.

Powell, G. Bingham and Guy D. Whitten. 1993. 'A Cross-National Analysis of Economic Voting: Taking Account of the Political Context'. *American Journal of Political Science* 37(2):391–414.

Rabinowitz, George and Stuart Elaine Macdonald. 1989. 'A Directional Theory of Issue Voting'. *American Political Science Review* 83(1):93–121.

Rabinowitz, George, James W. Prothro, and William Jacoby. 1982. 'Salience as a Factor in the Impact of Issues on Candidate Evaluation'. *The Journal of Politics* 44(1):41–63.

Rahn, Wendy M., Jon A. Krosnick, and Marijke Breuning. 1994. 'Rationalization and Derivation Processes in Survey Studies of Political Candidate Evaluation'. *American Journal of Political Science* 38(3):582–600.

Rand, Ayn. 1943. *The Fountainhead*. Indianapolis: Bobbs Merril.

RePass, David. E. 1971. 'Issue Salience and Party Choice'. *American Political Science Review* 65(2):389–400.

Robertson, David. 1976. *Theory of Party Competition*. London: Wiley.

Roller, Edeltraud. 1998. 'Positions- und performanzbasierte Sachfragenorientierungen und Wahlentscheidung: Eine theoretische und empirische Analyse aus Anlass der Bundestagswahl 1994'. In *Wahlen und Wähler. Analysen aus Anlass der Bundestagswahl 1994*, ed. Max Kaase and Hans-Dieter Klingemann. Wiesbaden: Westdeutscher Verlag, pp. 173–219.

Rose, Richard and Ian McAllister. 1986. *Voters Begin to Choose: From Closed-Class to Open Elections in Britain*. Beverly Hills: Sage.

Ruedin, Didier. 2013. 'Obtaining Party Positions on Immigration in Switzerland: Comparing Different Methods'. *Swiss Political Science Review* 19(1):84–105.

Sanders, David. 1999. 'The Impact of Left Right-Ideology'. In *Critical Elections: British Parties and Voters in Long-Term Perspective*, ed. Geoffrey Evans and Pippa Norris. London: Sage, pp. 181–206.

Sanders, David, Harold Clarke, Marianne Stewart, and Paul Whiteley. 2001. 'The Economy and Voting'. *Parliamentary Affairs* 54(4):789–802.

Seeberg, Henrik Bech. 2016. 'How Stable Is Political Parties' Issue Ownership? A Cross-Time, Cross-National Analysis'. *Political Studies* 65(2):475–492.

Sellers, Patrick J. 1998. 'Strategy and Background in Congressional Campaigns'. *American Political Science Review* 92(1):159–171.

Shapiro, Michael J. 1969. 'Rational Political Man: A Synthesis of Economic and Social-Psychological Perspectives'. *American Political Science Review* 63(4):1106–1119.

Sides, John. 2006. 'The Origins of Campaign Agendas'. *British Journal of Political Science* 36(3):407–436.

Simon, Adam F. 2002. *The Winning Message: Candidate Behavior, Campaign Discourse, and Democracy*. Cambridge: Cambridge University Press.

Spoon, Jae-Jae and Heike Klüver. 2014. 'Do Parties Respond? How Electoral Context Influences Party Responsiveness'. *Electoral Studies* 35:48–60.

Stokes, Donald E. 1963. 'Spatial Models of Party Competition'. *American Political Science Review* 57(2):368–377.

Stokes, Donald E. 1985. 'The Paradox of Campaign Appeals and Election Mandates'. *Proceedings of the American Philosophical Society* 129(1):20–25.

Stokes, Donald E. 1992. 'Valence Politics'. In *Electoral Politics*, ed. Dennis Kavanagh. Oxford: Clarendon Press, pp. 141–164.

Stubager, Rune. 2018. 'What Is Issue Ownership and How Should We Measure It?' *Political Behavior* 40(2):345–370.

Stubager, Rune and Henrik Bech Seeberg. 2016. 'What Can a Party Say? How Parties' Communication Can Influence Voters' Issue Ownership Perceptions'. *Electoral Studies* 44:162–171.

Stubager, Rune and Rune Slothuus. 2013. 'What Are the Sources of Political Parties Issue Ownership? Testing Four Explanations at the Individual Level'. *Political Behavior* 35(3):567–588.

Swalve, Tilko, Thomas Bräuninger, and Nathalie Giger. 2017. 'Polarized Perceptions: The Individual Perception of Ideological Scales in the U.S. Mass Public'. *Working Paper*.

Taber, Charles S. and Milton Lodge. 2006. 'Motivated Skepticism in the Evaluation of Political Beliefs'. *American Journal of Political Science* 50(3):755–769.

Taylor, Michael and Valentine M. Herman. 1971. 'Party Systems and Government Stability'. *American Political Science Review* 65(1):28–37.

Therriault, Andrew. 2015. 'Whose Issue Is It Anyway? A New Look at the Meaning and Measurement of Issue Ownership'. *British Journal of Political Science* 45(4):929–938.

Tillman, Erik R. 2008. 'Economic Judgments, Party Choice, and Voter Abstention in Cross-National Perspective'. *Comparative Political Studies* 41(9):1290–1309.

Tomz, Michael and Robert P. Van Houweling. 2008. 'Candidate Positioning and Voter Choice'. *American Political Science Review* 102(3):303–318.

Tresch, Anke and Alexandra Feddersen. 2019. 'The (In)stability of Voters' Perceptions of Competence and Associative Issue Ownership: The Role of Media Campaign Coverage'. *Political Communication* 36(3): 394–411.

Tresch, Anke, Jonas Lefevere, and Stefaan Walgrave. 2015. ' "Steal Me If You Can!": The Impact of Campaign Messages on Associative Issue Ownership'. *Party Politics* 21(2):198–208.

Tresch, Anke, Pascal Sciarini, and Frederic Varone. 2013. 'The Relationship between Media and Political Agendas: Variations across Decision-Making Phases'. *West European Politics* 36(5):897–918.

van Buuren, Stef and Karin Groothuis-Oudshoorn. 2011. 'mice: Multivariate Imputation by Chained Equations in R'. *Journal of Statistical Software* 45(3):1–67.

van Buuren, Stef, Karin Groothuis-Oudshoorn, Alexander Robitzsch, Gerko Vink, Lisa Doove, and Shahab Jolani. 2016. *Package mice*.

van der Brug, W. 2017. 'Issue Ownership: An Ambiguous Concept'. In *The Sage Handbook of Electoral Behaviour*, ed. Kai Arzheimer, Jocelyn Evans, and Michael S. Lewis-Beck. Los Angeles, CA: Sage, pp. 521–537.

van der Brug, Wouter. 2004. 'Issue Ownership and Party Choice'. *Electoral Studies* 23(2):209–233.

van der Eijk, Cees. 2001. 'Measuring Agreement in Ordered Rating Scales'. *Quality and Quantity* 35(3):325–341.

van der Eijk, Cees, Wouter Van der Brug, Martin Kroh, and Mark Franklin. 2006. 'Rethinking the Dependent Variable in Voting Behavior: On the Measurement and Analysis of Electoral Utilities'. *Electoral Studies* 25:424–447.

Volkens, Andrea, Pola Lehmann, Theres Matthiess, Nicolas Merz, Sven Regel, and Bernhard Wessels. 2017. *The Manifesto Data Collection. Manifesto Project (MRG/CMP/MARPOR). Version 2017a.* Berlin: Wissenschaftszentrum Berlin für Sozialforschung (WBZ).

Wagner, Markus and Eva Zeglovits. 2014. 'Survey Questions about Party Competence: Insights from Cognitive Interviews'. *Electoral Studies* 34:280–290.

Walgrave, Stefaan, Anke Tresch, and Jonas Lefevere. 2015. 'The Conceptualisation and Measurement of Issue Ownership'. *West European Politics* 38(4):778–796.

Walgrave, Stefaan and Jonas Lefevere. 2017. 'Long-Term Associative Issue Ownership Change: A Panel Study in Belgium'. *Journal of Elections, Public Opinion and Parties* 27(4):484–502.

Walgrave, Stefaan, Jonas Lefevere, and Anke Tresch. 2012. 'The Associative Dimension of Issue Ownership'. *The Public Opinion Quarterly* 76(4):771–782.

Walgrave, Stefaan, Jonas Lefevere, and Anke Tresch. 2014. 'The Limits of Issue Ownership Dynamics: The Constraining Effect of Party Preferences'. *Journal of Elections, Public Opinion and Parties* 24(1):1–19.

Walgrave, Stefaan, Jonas Lefevere, and Michiel Nuytemans. 2009. 'Issue Ownership Stability and Change: How Political Parties Claim and Maintain Issues through Media Appearances'. *Political Communication* 26(2):153–172.

Walgrave, Stefaan, Kirsten Van Camp, Jonas Lefevere, and Anke Tresch. 2016. 'Measuring Issue Ownership with Survey Questions. A Question Wording Experiment'. *Electoral Studies* 42:290–299.

Walgrave, Stefaan and Knut De Swert. 2007. 'Where Does Issue Ownership Come from? From the Party or from the Media? Issue-Party Identifications in Belgium, 1991–2005'. *International Journal of Press/Politics* 12(1):37–67.

Ward, Dalston, Jeong Hyun Kim, Matthew Graham, and Margit Tavits. 2015. 'How Economic Integration Affects Party Issue Emphases'. *Comparative Political Studies* 48(10):1227–1259.

Westholm, Anders. 1997. 'Distance versus Direction: The Illusory Defeat of the Proximity Theory of Electoral Choice'. *American Political Science Review* 91(4):865–883.

Wlezien, Christopher. 2005. 'On the Salience of Political Issues: The Problem with "Most Important Problem"'. *Electoral Studies* 24(4):555–579.

Zaller, John. 1992. *The Nature and Origins of Mass Opinion*. Cambridge: Cambridge University Press.

Index

About the Author

Simon Lanz is a political scientist trained at the University of Zurich and the University of Geneva. His research focuses on political behaviour in elections and direct democratic votes, comparative politics, and quantitative methods.

In 2017, he defended his doctoral thesis on issue ownership voting. The thesis won the award from the School of Social Sciences at the University of Geneva for the best PhD of 2017. In 2019, he received the prize of the Swiss Political Science Association for the best dissertation (years 2017 and 2018). As a recipient of the grant 'Politikstipendium'Simon worked for the Social Security and Health Committees at the Swiss Parliament (2018 and 2019). As of November 2019, he works for the Swiss Federal Social Insurance Office.

www.ingramcontent.com/pod-product-compliance
Lightning Source LLC
Chambersburg PA
CBHW020004290326
41935CB00007B/295